WITHDRAWN

D1649421

LOUIS NOWRA was born in Melbourne. He is the author of such plays as *Inner Voices, Visions, Inside the Island, The Precious Woman, Sunrise, The Golden Age, Capricornia, Byzantine Flowers, The Watchtower, Summer of the Aliens, Cosi, Radiance, The Temple, Crow, Miss Bosnia, The Incorruptible, The Jungle* and *The Language of the Gods*. He has written a non-fiction work *The Cheated*, three novels *The Misery of Beauty, Palu, Red Nights* and a memoir *The Twelfth of Never*. Some of his radio plays include *The Song Room, The Widows, Sydney, Moon of the Exploding Trees* and *The Divine Hammer*. Besides translating such plays as *The Prince of Homburg, Cyrano de Bergerac* and *Lulu*, he has written the libretti for *Whitsunday* and *Love Burns*. Telemovies are *Displaced Persons, Hunger* and *The Lizard King*. He wrote the screenplays for *Map of the Human Heart, Cosi, Heaven's Burning* and *Radiance*. He lives in Sydney.

THE LEARNING RESOURCE CENTRE
HERSCHEL GRAMMAR SCHOOL
NORTHAMPTON AVENUE
SLOUGH       SL1 3BW

To Gerri Williams and Adam Cook. And, of course, Hilary Linstead - who was right all along.

*Mozart was probably one of the sanest people who ever lived except for his preoccupation with scatology and his obsession that his wife may have been unfaithful to him*

Joseph Feher
*The Problem of Constanze Mozart's Fidelity*

LEARNING RESOURCE CENTRE
HERSCHEL GRAMMAR SCHOOL
NORTHAMPTON AVENUE
SLOUGH
SL1 3BW

# Così

## LOUIS NOWRA

CURRENCY PRESS • SYDNEY

CURRENCY PLAYS

First published in 1992 by
Currency Press Pty Ltd
PO Box 2287
Strawberry Hills NSW 2012
www.currency.com.au
enquiries@currency.com.au

This revised edition published in 1994
Reprinted 1995 (twice), 1996, 1997 (twice), 1998 (twice), 1999, 2000, 2001, 2002, 2003

Copyright © Louis Nowra, 1994, *Così, Trial by Madmen*; Gerry Turcotte, 1994, *Frankenstein's Mozart: The Making of Così*.

Copying for Educational Purposes:
The Australian *Copyright Act* 1968 allows a maximum of one chapter or 10% of this book, whichever is the greater, to be copied by any educational institution for its educational purposes provided that the educational institution (or the body that administers it) has given a remuneration notice to Copyright Agency Limited (CAL) under the Act. For details of the CAL licence for educational institutions please contact CAL, 19/157 Liverpool Street, Sydney, NSW 2000, tel (02) 9394 7600, fax (02) 9394 7601, email: info@copyright.com.au.

Copying for Other Purposes:
Except as permitted under the Act, for example a fair dealing for the purposes of study, research, criticism or review, no part of this book may be reproduced, stored in a retrieval system, or transmitted in any form or by any means without prior written permission. All inquiries should be made to the publisher at the above address.

Any performance or public reading of *Così* is forbidden unless a licence has been received from the author or the author's agent. The purchase of this book in no way gives the purchaser the right to perform the play in public, whether by means of a staged production or a reading. All applications for public performance should be made to the author, c/o HLA Management, PO Box 1536, Strawberry Hills NSW 2012, email hla@hlamgt.com.au.

NATIONAL LIBRARY OF AUSTRALIA CIP DATA
Nowra, Louis, 1950–
    *Così*
    New ed.
    ISBN 0 86819 403 4
    I. Title
    A822.3
Cover design Trevor Hood
Cover photos by Stuart Spence
Front cover shows Barry Otto and Ben Mendelsohn; back cover shows the closing scene. Both photos from the Belvoir Street Production.
Printed by Southwood Press, Marrickville NSW

This publication has been assisted by the Commonwealth Government through the Australia Council, its arts funding and advisory body.

# CONTENTS

# Frankenstein's Mozart: The Making of *Così*

## Gerry Turcotte

Havelock Ellis once wrote, 'Every artist writes his own autobiography', and with *Così* it is tempting to conclude that Louis Nowra has made the transition to such writing, a process begun with *Summer of the Aliens*. Indeed, there are numerous parallels between the life of the artist and that of the central character of these plays, not the least of which is the protagonist's name—Lewis. Of course, referring to *Aliens* and *Così* as autobiographical plays ignores two major factors. One is that earlier plays have always revolved around what Nowra has called 'a hidden ... powerful undercurrent of emotional autobiography', which is what Ellis was really driving at. And the other is that one does well to remember, as Clive James insists, that 'Autobiography is a lying art'.

Nowra himself makes use of the image of Doctor Frankenstein to explain the process of autobiographical (re)construction. Each situation, each character, each emotion which surfaces in a particular text is drawn together from a myriad collection of differently and imperfectly remembered situations. And the very act of re-membering—of putting the Frankenstein's monster of the past together—is an act of subterfuge, of legerdermain, of crafty artifice. As Northrop Frye puts it, 'Most autobiographies are inspired by a creative, and therefore *fictional* impulse, to select only those events and experiences in the writer's life that go to build up an integrated pattern'.[1] Autobiography is at once deceitful and honestly revealing. One Australian critic has claimed that it 'is both a form of striptease and an archaeology of the self'.[2] Or, in

Nowra's words, 'What I have done is act like Frankenstein. Like the doctor I have raided the graveyard of my memory and have created a monster out of the various limbs and appendages I could dig up.'

Although it may be difficult, if not ultimately futile, to try to establish where 'truth' and 'fiction' intersect, it is certainly possible to reflect on the change of direction Nowra's work is taking. In an act of parochiality, Nowra was attacked early in his career for not setting his plays in Australia—and hence for not dealing with 'homegrown' issues. He was also criticised for painting on very large canvasses, turning to Paraguay or Russia for his settings, or probing the effects of imperialism through sweeping plays such as *The Precious Woman* and *Visions*. At the heart of both critiques was an inability on the part of many critics to see that Nowra was in fact incisively investigating his own culture, through metaphor, through parable and of course by inference.

Now that such accusations are less likely to be levelled, Nowra has ironically changed his emphasis. He has moved firmly onto Australian soil, and he has moved away from the large character studies of the past—as we find in *Sunrise* and *Capricornia* for example—to detail with frightening precision the tragedy and humour of everyday lives, through more intimate studies.

In *Aliens* and *Così* , the scalpel moves closer to the personal vein, and it also reveals a lighter side to Nowra's traditionally 'Gothic' vision—Frankenstein has a sense of humour, as it were. Not that his work has been without levity. But it is true to say that despite an often oblique sense of hopefulness, by and large Nowra's plays have been dark: Juana goes mad in *Visions*, Ivan returns to the prison of his mind in *Inner Voices*, and the fire rages ever closer in *Sunrise*. Even *The Golden Age* suggests the inability of humanity to pull itself together, and by extension, the fate of his major characters seems sealed.

There is an entirely different 'feel', however, to his more recent plays. Act One of *Radiance* is euphoric, although it hints towards a tragedy to come. *The Temple*, Nowra's most commercially successful play, is positively, frantically, comic. And in *Summer of the Aliens*, though particularly in *Così*, Nowra seems to hit a perfect register, using humour to move the plays along and to reflect critically on what is often a tragedy of human suffering. Not to put too strong a term to it, Nowra's humour in these recent plays is almost redemptive. It exposes weakness and stupidity, and, in Mordecai Richler's phrase, 'it ridicules our prejudices and popular institutions'—but it is not exploitative or gratuitous. The comic element here suggests a level of commensurability that links the suffering and existence of a wide range of individuals.

And it is this sense of commensurability of experience which anchors what is surely an absurd proposition: that a group of intellectually or emotionally handicapped individuals could mount a production of Mozart's *Così Fan Tutte*. A cynic would say that this is the profile of any successful theatrical ensemble, although Nowra's digs seem targetted chiefly at directors. Roy—a manic-depressive visionary—is given the best of such lines. At one stage he maintains that, 'All directors are tyrants', and at another he tells Lewis, 'For killing an actor he'd get life, for killing a director he'd get eternal gratitude'.

The premise of *Così*, then, is that a young, first-time director, is hired to direct a play as part of a therapeutic program meant to keep the inmates of an asylum interested, and to 'bring them out of their shells', as Justin, a social worker, puts it. Unfortunately for Lewis, Roy has decided on Mozart's *Così Fan Tutte*, not just an *opera buffa*, but an Italian one. Of course, none of the few volunteers can speak Italian much less sing—indeed, some can barely speak. To make matters worse, the venue for this performance is a fire-gutted theatre with a leaking roof and faulty wiring. The cast includes a pyromaniac, a junkie, a knife-wielding romantic, a confused realist, a Lithium-addicted pianist who hates Mozart, and a stuttering ex-lawyer who refuses to take part in the production. Lewis, needless to say, is slightly discouraged by the task at hand.

In *Così*, the burnt-out stage is a metaphor for the world at large, and the drama which is enacted on its charred surface is a reflection of the larger drama taking place outside. In *Summer of the Aliens*, the Cuban missile crisis acts as the register for a world on the brink of disaster against which are played the smaller though no less important dramas of Lewis and Dulcie's coming-of-age, Pisano's madness and Norma's dead-end life and marriage. In *Così*, it is the 1970s, and the Vietnam war frames the drama. As Peter Ward has argued in a recent review, as the production of *Così* develops, 'the war and anti-war themes on the edge of the action's focus become a madness without, enclosing saner, if flawed, aspirations within'.[3] Along the same lines, Frank Gauntlett has claimed that, 'when Louis Nowra places his fruitcake-rich, riotously funny, beautifully conceived play *Così* in a Melbourne madhouse he has less to say about life within the rubber walls than without'.[4]

There are numerous elements of *Così* which are vintage Nowra: the use of an external threat to texture and enrich the principal drama; the device of the play-within-a-play to create resonant ironies; even the juxtaposition of sanity and insanity to question and trouble the problematic nature of what is considered normal. As to the latter, in *Inner Voices* greed and violence are the values inscribed on the *tabula rasa* of Ivan's mind; and in *The Golden Age*, the so-called 'inferior' remnants of lost Europeans are effectively killed off in a Tasmanian mental institution which is meant to be their salvation. In each case, and again in *Così*, Nowra forces his audience to question what it means exactly to be 'normal', by showing that often the 'troubled' vision of his 'abnormal' characters is perhaps clearer and saner than those outside the institutions.

Mozart's *Così Fan Tutte* is an inspired choice as the centrepiece for the drama. For one thing, the enormity of the task makes the comedy that much stronger. For another, the aristocratic nature of the opera, combined with its frivolity and sexism, play well into many of the issues which Nowra's contemporary drama pursues. This is Roy's summary of the opera:

> It starts off in a coffee shop in Naples. Italy. These two fellows are boasting how faithful their girlfriends are. So this old fellow, Don Alfonso, says to Guglielmo and Ferrando, okay, let's make a wager and test the girls' fidelity. So the young men pretend to go off to war, but they really don't. Instead they disguise themselves as Albanians and woo the girls.... The girls won't fall for the Albanians and so they pretend to suicide and guess what? ... Guglielmo's girlfriend falls for Ferrando and vice versa. Anyway, the boys reveal their disguises and things right themselves and Don Alfonso is proved right. Women are never true. Hence the title *Così Fan Tutte*: Women are like that.
>
> (Act One, Scene one)

*Così Fan Tutte* is considered by some to be the ideal of *opera buffa*, or comic opera. Completed in January of 1790, it was said to be inspired both by actual events as well as by Mozart's own distress over his inconstant wife. Although considered by many contemporary critics as 'Mozart's most sumptuously beautiful opera',[5] it was also described, in its day, as a scandalous piece. As Alfred Einstein puts it, 'No work of Mozart's has experienced such opposition and occasioned so many attempts to 'rescue' it as *Così fan tutte*'.[6]

Lewis's mismatched players, one could say, are yet more in a long line of rescuers, re-writing the libretto, and reinvesting the performance so that it reflects their own needs. Ironically, the production of *Così* is opposed in much the same way that it was when it was first composed, although the reasons are different. In the 1790s the opera was considered immoral; in the 1970s it is a symbol of sexist attitudes, and a decadent indulgence in bourgeois romanticism, at a time of protest and political agitation. In fact, Lewis's flatmates criticise him for talking about love, not war. As Lewis explains to one of the inmates, his girlfriend 'hates me doing an opera about love and fidelity while thousands of Vietnamese are being killed by American troops.'

In its original form, *Così* ran to three and a half hours, and moved between the burnt-out theatre and Lewis's rented house beside a slaughterhouse. The play has been trimmed so that all the action now takes place in what is a veritable theatre of the absurd, a shell of a place which perhaps even hints at the destruction wrought by war. Lewis's act of bringing Mozart's 'music of the spheres' to life in such a sterile place, rather than Bertolt Brecht's politically correct *The Exception and the Rule*, is an act of inspired madness that suggests the insane potential of individuals to rise above the so-called rationality of war, formulaic thinking and ordinariness. Perhaps Roy's dream for the opera says it best:

> I had a dream.... There would be music, music of the spheres, colourful costumes, joie de vivre, a world that was as far removed from this depressing asylum as possible. A world that was like my childhood.... That's the world I wanted *Così Fan Tutte* to capture—recapture. But it's gone, the music too.
> (Act Two, Scene One)

Louis Nowra's *Così* brings the music back to life.

University of Wollongong, 1994.

1. Northrop Frye, *Anatomy of Criticism*, New York, 1968, 307. Italics added.
2. John Colmer, *Australian Autobiography: the Personal Quest*, Oxford, Oxford University Press, 1989, 7.
3. 'Cosi', *The Australian*, Friday, July 23, 1993, p.12.
4. *Telegraph Mirror*, 23 April 1992.
5. See, for example, Henry Raynor, *Mozart*, London: Macmillan, 1978, p.116.
6. Alfred Einstein, *Mozart: His Character, His Work*, trans. Arthur Mendel and Nathan Broder, Great Britain: Panther, 1977, p.459.

# Trial by Madmen

## Louis Nowra

Written at probably one of the most intensely difficult periods of my life, *Così* is one of my most lighthearted plays. Each morning when I climbed the ladder to my South Melbourne attic I had never felt keener on entering the world of one of my plays. Like *Summer of the Aliens, Così* is partly auto-biographical. Both centre on a character called Lewis (there, but for a vowel could be me). *Summer of the Aliens* was Lewis at fourteen, *Così* is Lewis at twenty-one. I suppose I chose those years because they were turning points in my understanding of people. Contrary to the opinions of those phrenologists of the 20th century - the psychiatrists - it is sometimes events and experiences after your youth that determine the way you view the world, and so it was with my experiences that are part of *Così*.

Both my grandmothers ended up in mental institutions. On my mother's side, grandmother undoubtedly was suffering from a form of senility. Having always prided herself on her mental abilities (she could recite, in order, all the kings and queens of England) she found herself falling into the darkness of mental illness. When I visited her in Mont Park asylum she seemed to me to be the same person, but more discursive and mentally unfocussed. There is a current theory that far from being like a computer, the brain resembles a jungle. If this is so, then grandmother's brain became an inpenetrable jungle, swallowing up any explorer who dared to enter. On my father's side my grandma deliberately chose madness as a way of dealing with the fact that her seventy-year-old husband had run off with a thirty-year-old barmaid. When I visited her in Mont Park (years after my other grandmother was in there) she lived permanently in the year 1948. As far as she was concerned, I did not exist, because I hadn't been born yet and to complicate matters she thought I was my father. When she asked if I were to marry my mother, not only could I give the date, but I could tell her how many children I would have and so on. Some people would say that in having to pretend I was my father about to marry my mother I was taking part in a Freudian nightmare, but I prefer to see it as my having fallen, like Alice, down a hole to end up in topsy turvy land.

So, unlike Lewis in *Così* I had experience of mental institutions. It is difficult to rediscover my motives for involving myself with mental patients. I suspect that the madness of my grandmothers gave me an intense interest in the subject. Madness both frightened and attracted me. This was 1971 and the era of R.D. Laing, a Scottish psychiatrist whose view of madness was oddly reassuring in a decade going crazy. One of his ideas was that labelling people mad was to stigmatise them, and that many mentally ill people should be allowed to go totally mad - once at rock bottom they would again find their true selves. This idea of true and false selves is such a philosophical, let alone a psychological flim-flam that it is not surprising that someone like myself, at twenty-one, was attracted to it. I even approached the mental health authority and proposed that I write a history of asylums in Victoria. Not having the intellectual rigour to do this, I decided to work with mental patients.

This was also the era when chemicals began to control many of the wilder excesses of madmen and saw the first influx of social workers, who like grass burrs, were attaching themselves onto our social fabric. One social worker asked a friend and myself if we wanted to do theatre with mental patients, 'to bring them out of their selves' (I suspect he meant 'shells'). Having the confidence and certainty of youth I thought that theatre would be therapeutic.

One of the connections I feel with Lewis now is my first day in rehearsals. Instead of feeling cocky, I felt a great terror. Facing so many faces, some earnest, shy and irritated, I suddenly realised I was responsible for these people. I wanted them to 'come out of their shells', but at the time feared what would happen.

So who was I then, and how much was I like Lewis? I was a person who was very much removed from what was around him. Working with mental patients seemed to me to be something to believe in, something far removed from the political rhetoric of the anti-Vietnam war protests of the late 1960s. Every day I would turn up at the Mont Park hall, to rehearse *Trial by Jury*. This was the added burden. I hated Gilbert and Sullivan but one of the patients wanted to do it. Some patients agreed with me and demanded more 'singable' songs, so we incorporated Beatles and Bee Gees songs into the show. As we rehearsed I realised that although I was working with the most approachable patients, many were mad. No trendy philosophy can hide the terrifying nature of madness for both the sufferer and his relatives.

Once I had gotten over any impulses to be a do-gooder I began to enjoy rehearsals. There was only one performance. Some relatives of the patients came, but the audience was mostly other patients. Before the performance started a student radical came along. Here was a fellow who preached revolution and the equality of all, and this radical, let's call him Nick, started to sing into the microphone, as patients filed in, the song about madness 'They're coming to take me away, ha, ha!' I had never felt such anger towards anyone in my life.

The show was probably terrible. A curious, eccentric mixture of original songs, rock and roll and Gilbert and Sullivan. Yet, afterwards in the changing rooms, I felt exhilarated, as did the patients. It is a feeling I sometimes experience when I go backstage after one of my plays; a mixture of giggling, hysteria, cockiness and relief. Like the patients, I wanted to do another play, but we never did.

Someone who saw the first production of *Così* complained that I was mocking the patients. Certainly I did not set out to do that. I also had no intention of adding to the modern cliche: people outside the asylum are more mad than those inside. But one thing I am proud of is how the shyer members of the *Trial by Jury* cast blossomed and gradually I lost any notion of Me and Them. *Così* is faintly based on that production and is a mixture of autobiography, fiction, and my more recent experiences.

Sydney, December 1993

*Così* was first performed by Company B at the Belvoir Street Theatre, Sydney on 21 April, 1992 with the following cast:

| | |
|---|---|
| HENRY | Bob Baines |
| JUSTIN, NICK, ZAC | David Field |
| LUCY, JULIE | Kerry Fox |
| CHERRY | Celia Ireland |
| RUTH | Elspeth MacTavish |
| LEWIS | Ben Mendelsohn |
| ROY | Barry Otto |
| DOUG | David Wenham |

Directed by Adam Cook
Designed by Stephen Curtis
Lighting by Mark Shelton

**Photograph Acknowledgements:** page vi from left -Philip Holder as Roy and Luciano Martucci as Lewis in The State Theatre Company of S.A. production of *Così*, 1993. Photographer: David Wilson. All other photographs are by Stuart Spence from the Belvoir Street production, 1992. Page vii Barry Otto (background) as Roy, David Field as Justin and Ben Mendelsohn as Lewis; page viii David Wenham as Doug; page 51 Ben Mendelsohn as Lewis and Kerry Fox as Julie; page 52 Bob Baines as Henry; page 53 Barry Otto as Roy; page 54 Barry Otto as Roy and Ben Mendelsohn as Lewis; page 55 Celia Ireland as Cherry and Ben Mendelsohn as Lewis; page 56 David Wenham as Doug and Celia Ireland as Cherry.

## CHARACTERS

LEWIS, 21, has just left university.

LUCY, 20-23, is doing an MA thesis and lives with Lewis.

NICK, 21-24, also doing a thesis and directs student productions.

JUSTIN, a social worker in his late 30s or early 40s. He is neat and precise.

ROY, 40-50, a mental patient who has spent much of his life in institutions.

HENRY, 40-50, a former lawyer who is now a patient. Like Roy, he has spent much of his adult life in institutions.

DOUG, 20-30, has a liking for fires, but has not been in institutions very long.

CHERRY, 25-35, has been in institutions for some time.

JULIE, 21-25, is in a mental institution for the first time because of drug dependency.

RUTH, 30-40, an obsessive personality, who is in and out of mental institutions.

ZAC, 25-30, the musician of the group who has been in and out of mental institutions.


## SETTING

The time is 1971. The play is set in a Melbourne mental institution.

# ACT ONE

## SCENE ONE

*A burnt out theatre. It is day outside but pitch black inside the theatre. A heavy door opens, a chink of daylight enters, as do three people:* LEWIS, *his girlfriend,* LUCY, *and his friend,* NICK.

LUCY: Where are the lights?

LEWIS: Don't know.

NICK: Maybe over there.

> [*The door slams shut.*]

Damn! [*fiddling with the lock*] Christ, it's locked from the inside.

LEWIS: I thought I saw a switch over there.

> [*They fumble in the darkness for a light switch.*]

NICK: Smells like it hasn't been used in years.

LUCY: Burnt wood and mould. Are you sure you know what you're doing?

LEWIS: I need the money, Lucy.

> [NICK *accidentally touches* LUCY *who cries out in alarm.*]

NICK: [*enjoying this*] It's a ghost.

LUCY: Nick, just find the light!

NICK: All theatres have ghosts.

LUCY: I can't believe you're going to do a show here.

NICK: Mad actors are bad enough, but madmen...

LEWIS: You said you were going to help me.

NICK: As long as you do *Galileo* with me.
LUCY: I wish you boys would learn to drive, I'm late for my
    tutorial.
    [*There is the sound of breaking glass.*]
NICK: [*nervously*] What's that?
LUCY: Someone's breaking in.
NICK: Who is it? Who's there?
ROY: [*nervously*] Is that you, Justin?
LEWIS: No.
ROY: Who is it? Who's there? Answer me!
LUCY: [*relieved*] Found it!
    [*The lights go on. A dismal hall is revealed. A silence as
    they stare at one another.*]
ROY: How did you get in?
LEWIS: The door.
ROY: It was locked when I checked it this morning. That's why
    I broke in. Didn't want to be late.
LEWIS: The superintendent gave me the key. Are you the social
    worker?
ROY: No, I'm a patient.
LUCY: I have to go now. See you at home, Lewis.
NICK: Lucy! Wait! I'm coming with you.
LEWIS: But you were going to help me.
NICK: [*taking him aside*] I will, but I just remembered I have to
    meet my thesis supervisor. He's on my back because I'm
    spending so much time organising the moratorium.
LUCY: Nick, I don't have much time.
NICK: Coming! [*To* LEWIS] Don't forget the *Galileo* rehearsals.
    [*He goes after* LUCY. LEWIS *feels betrayed. He and* ROY, *shy
    of one another are silent until* ROY *decides to break it.*]
ROY: This is where I belong: in the theatre.
    [LEWIS *nods, not knowing what to say.* JUSTIN ANDERSON
    *enters.*]
JUSTIN: Morning, Roy. [*To* LEWIS] And what ward are you
    from?
LEWIS: I'm not from a ward. I'm the director--

JUSTIN: Lewis Riley?

LEWIS: Yes.

ROY: I was expecting someone a bit older.

JUSTIN: Justin Anderson. Everyone calls me Justin. I'm the social worker who initiated this project.

LEWIS: [looking at the theatre] It's burnt.

JUSTIN: Coat of paint and it'll be fine.

DOUG: [entering] Hey, someone must have been in here before me.

[He casts an expert eye on the damage.]

Allowed the fire brigade plenty of time to get here. Must have been kids.

JUSTIN: I thought you were in C ward?

DOUG: First person to have ever escaped from the closed ward since that murderer. [He notices JUSTIN's expression of horror] Having you on.

[HENRY enters. He is very quiet and never looks anyone in the eye. His left arm is paralysed and he carries it as if it were in an invisible sling.]

JUSTIN: Hello, Henry. You want to be in the play too?

[He says nothing and sits on a chair.]

ROY: Henry's part of my hand picked team.

DOUG: We're the only ones who answered your ad.

ROY: [paying no attention to DOUG] Wonder where the girls are?

[HENRY shakes his head.]

JUSTIN: [introducing ROY] This is Roy, one of the patients who came up with the idea of doing a show.

ROY: [shaking hands] We're going to make a great team. What's your name?

LEWIS: Lewis.

ROY: We'll be like Jerry Lewis and Dean Martin.

[JUSTIN guides LEWIS away from the enthusiastic ROY.]

JUSTIN: [sotto voce] He loves the theatre apparently. A great enthusiast when he gets going. He has his down periods like a lot of people, but he's your support, your natural energiser. And this is Doug.

DOUG: So you're the director?

LEWIS: [*uncomfortably*] Yes.

DOUG: Done anything I might have seen?

LEWIS: Probably not.

DOUG: You're bragging. What about a movie? Done a movie?

LEWIS: No.

DOUG: Poofter?

JUSTIN: Doug!

DOUG: I want to know just in case he puts the hard word on me like Dr Simpson.

JUSTIN: And Henry.

> [LEWIS *goes to shake hands with him but* HENRY *turns away.*]

Bit shy, the old Henry. Part of this project is to bring out people like Henry.

ROY: Shall we start now, Jerry?

JUSTIN: Hold your horses, we're waiting for the women. How many are there?

ROY: Great response, great response. We need only three and we got them.

JUSTIN: They take longer to get here because they have to come from the women's ward which is over the hill.

ROY: Where's the piano? Asylums are the most inefficient places on this earth.

DOUG: And when you want a lobotomy, you just can't get it, can you, Henry? Nod your head for a yes. Brilliant choice, Roy. Who does Henry play? A hero suffering from verbal diarrhoea.

JUSTIN: Doug!

DOUG: [*referring to* ROY] Mr Show Business here chose him.

ROY: Go burn a cat.

> [JUSTIN *sees* LEWIS's *apprehension and takes him aside.*]

JUSTIN: You must feel a bit queasy. I know I was when I first came to work in an asylum. The thing is, and you'll discover this, is that they are just normal people, well, not quite normal, or else they wouldn't be in here, would they? But you get my drift?

LEWIS: [*uncertainly*] Yes.

JUSTIN: They are normal people who have done extraordinary things, thought extraordinary thoughts. You are getting a good bunch. They'll be no real trouble: no carving knife against the throat. [*A beat*] You might want to keep a close eye on Doug, though. I didn't know he had been released from a closed ward – being in C ward means the patient is never allowed out, day or night, until we're satisfied they won't harm others or themselves. But he should be all right if they've let him out – as long as he's taking his medication. He's a bit cheeky the way he won't take it sometimes.

LEWIS: Is this where we're performing?

JUSTIN: It looks a bit dispirited, I know –

DOUG: [*shouting over to* LEWIS] You get to fuck the actresses?

JUSTIN: Doug!

DOUG: I was told that's why people want to direct.

JUSTIN: [*to* LEWIS] The government bought the land next to the asylum last year and this theatre was on it. Someone set fire to it, but it's safe. A bit grungy, as we say, but safe. There's some lights up there – what do you call them in the theatre?

[LEWIS *shakes his head.*]

Anyway, we'll get someone on the staff to have a look at the wiring.

[*He stares at the ceiling.*]

Bit of a hole up there. Let's hope it doesn't rain on the night, eh? [*A beat.*] Any questions?

LEWIS: What if someone forgets to take their medicine and –

JUSTIN: Goes berserk? That's for the movies. They'll just act a bit extraordinary, that's all. If something happens get someone to call a nurse. [*Looking at his watch*] I wish the women would hurry up.

LEWIS: What sort of thing do you want me to do with them?

JUSTIN: A play. I thought you had been told.

LEWIS: No, I mean, what sort of play?

JUSTIN: Up to you. A panto? Excerpts from Shakespeare. Whatever you like. The important thing is to keep them interested. To bring them out of their shells. Give them something interesting to do.

[*The lights start flickering.*]

Oh, oh, trouble in the fuse box.

[*He goes to examine it.*]

DOUG: [*to* LEWIS] So, where do you live?

LEWIS: Excuse me?

DOUG: Digs. Flat. House. Burrow. Abode. Shack.

LEWIS: I live in a house.

DOUG: Ah, nice. A house is a nice thing to live in. Where?

LEWIS: Where?

DOUG: You're not deaf, are you? The last thing we want is a deaf director. So what district? Suburb? Locale?

LEWIS: Northcote.

DOUG: What street?

LEWIS: Near the abattoirs.

DOUG: Oh, yeah, bit of a whiff in the morning?

LEWIS: It stinks all right.

DOUG: Cattle? Pigs?

LEWIS: Pigs.

DOUG: Scream a lot?

LEWIS: Sometimes.

[*Pause.*]

DOUG: Shacked up with a few sheilas, are you?

LEWIS: No.

DOUG: So, you're a poof?

ROY: About bloody time!

[CHERRY, RUTH *and* JULIE *enter.*]

CHERRY: It's a long walk.

DOUG: Do you good, you can lose some weight.

CHERRY: Go burn a cat.

JUSTIN: Doug! Cherry! [*A beat.*] Cherry, this is Lewis, our director.

LEWIS: [*shaking her hand*] Hello.

CHERRY: [*referring to his weak grip*] I'm not fragile.

JUSTIN: Lewis, this is Ruth.

RUTH: [*softly*] Hello.

JUSTIN: And... I'm sorry, I don't know your name.

JULIE: Julie.

DOUG: Detoxed yet?

JUSTIN: I want you on your best behaviour.

DOUG: What have I done now?

JUSTIN: Lewis, they all have to be back in their wards at four. Love to be here, but I've got a day of meetings. Rush, rush. Where would the world be without social workers?

DOUG: In tip top condition.

[HENRY *smiles.*]

JUSTIN: [*sotto voce to* LEWIS] Whenever this place gets too much for me, I always think of this definition – a madman is someone who arrives at a fancy dress party dressed in the Emperor's new clothes. You'll find it's a help to remember that.

[*Far from helping* LEWIS *it totally confuses him.*]

[*To everyone*] I'm off – break a leg!

[*He goes.*]

CHERRY: Do all social workers have a black sense of humour?

ROY: [*exasperated*] It's theatre talk, you drongo.

[*There is a long silence. Everyone is shy and they are waiting for some leadership from* LEWIS *who, stuck in these strange circumstances, doesn't know where to begin.*]

LEWIS: [*hesitantly*] This is an unusual position for me . . . I directed some plays at university . . . and, well . . . this is my first year out –

ROY: [*impatiently*] Come on, Jerry, let's get this show on the road.

[HENRY *gets up to go.* ROY *addresses him as if he were a dog.*]

Stay. Stay, Henry.

[HENRY *sits down again.* ROY *turns back to* LEWIS.]

So, we'll start now?

LEWIS: Yes, I guess it really gets down to what we want to do. I'm open. It looks like a small cast. We could do *The Exception and the Rule*. It's a play by Bertolt Brecht, a German playwright.

DOUG: What's it about?

LEWIS: How a man sacrifices himself for the good of his mates.

DOUG: I don't want to do any Christian plays.

LEWIS: No, it's not a Christian play, it's –

ROY: No, no, no! We're wasting time. I've already chosen what we're doing. *Così Fan Tutte*.

> [*Nobody has really heard of it.* HENRY *gets up to go.*]

Henry!

> [HENRY *obediently sits.*]

DOUG: We're going to perform it?

ROY: Yes.

DOUG: It's only a couple of minutes long.

ROY: It's three hours long, drongo. It's an opera.

DOUG: Little Richard wrote an opera? Can you beat that. Tutti Frutti, the opera. [*To* HENRY] What in the hell did he turn 'Good Golly, Miss Molly' into – a symphony?

ROY: Will you be quiet. *Così Fan Tutte* is an opera by Mozart. It's the greatest opera in the whole world. You'd be intimate with it, wouldn't you, Jerry? You're university educated.

LEWIS: [*plainly not intimate with it*] Mozart is not one of my big –

ROY: Favourites? But he will be, he will be.

CHERRY: What's it about?

ROY: About testing how true your true love is.

DOUG: Well, I'm shattered and wrung out already. And this goes on for three hours?

ROY: Shut up, or I'll knock your block off.

DOUG: [*shaping up*] Come on then.

CHERRY: [*yelling*] Doug! Roy! Stop, or I'll knock your block off! [*They calm down.*]

> [*Smiling, to* LEWIS] You have to be firm with them.

LEWIS: Let's hear the story.

ROY: [*to* LEWIS, *about* DOUG] A psychopath is too kind a word to describe him. [*A beat.*] It starts off in a coffee shop in Naples. Italy. These two fellows are boasting how faithful their girlfriends are. So this old fellow, Don Alfonso, says to Guglielmo and Ferrando, okay, let's make a wager and test the girls' fidelity. So the young men pretend to go off to war, but they really don't. Instead they disguise themselves as Albanians and woo the girls. [*Half to himself*] Kills me every time.

> [ROY *chuckles to himself at the humour of this plot twist, not noticing that* LEWIS, *like* CHERRY *and* DOUG *are becoming depressed at the triteness of the story.* HENRY *takes out a toy soldier and plays with it.*]

The girls won't fall for the Albanians and so they pretend to suicide and guess what?

CHERRY: The girls fall for the Albanians.

ROY: [*surprised she knew*] Yes. Yes. But there's another twist. Guglielmo's girlfriend falls for Ferrando and vice versa. Anyway, the boys reveal their disguises and things right themselves and Don Alfonso is proved right. Women are never true. Hence the title *Così Fan Tutte*: Women are like that.

> [*There is a long silence.* ROY *has not sold the story very well.*]

There's music, of course.

> [HENRY *gets up to leave. Without taking his eyes off* LEWIS, ROY *trips* HENRY, *who sprawls on the floor.* LEWIS *is horrified, but no one else takes any notice.*]

Some great music.

> [HENRY *sits down again.*]

Any questions?

LEWIS: Do you think we should be doing something like this?

ROY: You don't want to do a masterpiece?

LEWIS: In these days, you know, the Vietnam war –

ROY: They can pretend to be going off to the Vietnam war! Now you're cooking.

LEWIS: I meant about the theme. Love is not so important nowadays.

ROY: [*looking at* LEWIS *as if he's mad*] What planet are you from?

RUTH: Will we have cappuccinos?

LEWIS: Sorry?

RUTH: On stage. How will we make the froth?

LEWIS: I don't quite follow.

RUTH: For the opening scene in the coffee shop we'll have to have a real cappuccino machine.

LEWIS: We don't have to have cappuccino.

RUTH: Good, I don't like them.

ROY: [*to* LEWIS] We should get occupational therapy on to making the costumes straight away.

RUTH: [*to* LEWIS] So we'll pretend?

[*He looks at her quizzically.*]

To drink coffee.

LEWIS: If we do it – yes.

RUTH: But what if I want to stir the froth into the coffee?

LEWIS: Maybe we'll have instant coffee.

RUTH: Did they have instant coffee in Mozart's day?

[*Both* ROY *and* LEWIS *are becoming exasperated.*]

ROY: It doesn't matter, Ruth.

RUTH: But I don't like instant coffee.

ROY: Jerry, tell her, you're the director.

[LEWIS *is out of his depth with* RUTH.]

[*To* RUTH] You're not in the scene. Only the men are in the coffee house scene.

[*To* DOUG *referring to* LEWIS.] He couldn't direct a poofter to a man's dunny.

[ZAC *enters looking soporific.* ROY *is pleased to see him.*]

Ah, the orchestra! Zac, this is the director of the show. Jerry, this is Zac.

LEWIS: It's Lewis.

ROY: To you maybe, but not to Dean Martin.

ZAC: [*looking for the piano*] Piano?

ROY: Not here yet.

> [*The words are trying to pierce the drug fog of* ZAC's *brain.*]

ZAC: Piano?

ROY: The piano is coming tomorrow.

> [ZAC *abruptly turns around and heads back to his ward.*]
> [*Shouting after him*] Tomorrow. It'll definitely be here tomorrow.

DOUG: [*half to himself*] How much Lithium is the poor bugger on?

ROY: [*explaining* ZAC's *behaviour to* LEWIS] Without a piano Zac is only a threepence.

CHERRY: This *Così Tutti* –

ROY: *Così Fan Tutte*

CHERRY: Thing is just another thing about the battle of the sexes?

ROY: I suppose so, if you could describe the Crusades as a sightseeing lark on the way to Jerusalem. Look, everyone, show some enthusiasm. This is a masterpiece. Ever since I was a child I've adored it. My mother played the music to me over and over. You can count the productions of it on one finger in Australia. Well, none probably. I haven't seen any. We'll be making history. Australian history. We'll bring culture to this place. You know what culture is for most Australians, Jerry? It's the stuff that grows on stale cheddar.

DOUG: I wish he were on Lithium.

CHERRY: Let me get this right. There's a bit of singing in the show?

ROY: It's all singing.

> [*Everyone is stunned.*]

CHERRY: But I can't sing.

ROY: When I put the notice up on the board I said it was an opera.

CHERRY: It said 'Who wants to have fun in the theatre?'

ROY: That was the heading, but didn't you read anything under it. [*A beat.*] You can't sing at all?

CHERRY: Not opera.

ROY: Lewis will train you.

LEWIS: Roy –

DOUG: I can't sing a note, and, as for Henry here, to get him to speak a word is a miracle.

ROY: I heard him humming the other day. He's a natural. My instinct for this is always right. [*Noticing* LEWIS's *downcast expression*] Chin up, Jerry, she'll be apples. Now one more thing.

[*A beat.*] Who speaks Italian?

CHERRY: What?

ROY: It's all in Italian.

> [HENRY *gets up to leave.*]

Henry!

> [*But* HENRY *doesn't stop this time. He goes.*]

DOUG: I'm with Henry.

> [*He goes.*]

ROY: But it's an easy language. Ask any Italian!

CHERRY: For once I agree with Doug.

> [*She goes.*]

ROY: [*in despair*] No, no, no –

LEWIS: Perhaps we should do something a bit more simple. A one act play or something. That Brecht, that's simple –

ROY: This is my dream, Jerry. My dream. [*Noticing* JULIE *and* RUTH *are still there*] Aren't you two rats going to desert the Titanic?

JULIE: I prefer this to the ward.

RUTH: What's the name again?

ROY: [*as if dealing with a simpleton*] Così Fan Tutte.

> [*He disconsolately flips through his treasured possession, the piano reduction of Così Fan Tutte.*]

LEWIS: [*trying to cheer him up*] Is that the music to it? [ROY *nods*] You wouldn't happen to have a record of it, would you?

ROY: It's all in my head. Without this, the world wouldn't be the same. It would break, like a voice in despair shattering glass. There is the harmony of the spheres and that harmony is Mozart's music. *Così Fan Tutte.* Without this opera having been composed, there would be just a clanging, banging, a bedlam all around us. The music of this opera keeps the world in harmony. [*Swinging back to optimistic determination*] I'll win them over, Jerry! Trust me. Tomorrow come back and you'll find we've missed the iceberg and are sailing in calm waters.

## SCENE TWO

*The theatre. Day.* RUTH *is singing to the simple, terminally slow playing of* ZAC. *She can hold a tune but is mechanical in performing and is nervous at the people watching her. She sings 'Wild Thing'.*

RUTH:                     Wild thing, you make my heart sing
                          Wild thing you make everything groovy . . .
       [*Everyone applauds at the end of the song.* ROY *is particularly enthusiastic.*]
ROY: That's it. That's the spirit.
       [*He looks to* LEWIS.]
LEWIS: I was hoping for a song that showed a greater vocal range.
RUTH: It's the only song I know all the way through. I'm not going to sing a song that is not word perfect. You don't want me to make a fool of myself, do you?
ROY: A definite if not the definitive Dorabella, don't you think, Jerry?
       [LEWIS *gives a tiny nod of the head, unable to believe he has found himself caught up in this.*]
LEWIS: Who's next?

ROY: Henry. Come on, Henry, you're the lucky last.

[HENRY *is reluctant and doesn't move from his seat.*]

Henry!

[*He drags* HENRY *from the chair.*]

Did your clients have to drag you up to defend them in court?

[*To* ZAC.] Play 'When you Wish upon a Star', everyone knows that.

[*Plainly,* ZAC *doesn't.* ROY *is irritated.*]

'When the Saints Go Marching In'.

[ZAC *plays a terminally slow version.*]

Henry, that's your intro.

HENRY: Cccccccan't ssssing.

[*He sits down. A long silence.*]

LEWIS: I don't think this is going to work, Roy.

[*A shiver of doubt momentarily possesses* ROY, *but it passes.*]

ROY: Jerry, I believe in Henry, he's the perfect Don Alfonso. Henry used to be a lawyer, they're all cynical, like Don Alfonso. And, look, Cherry's a natural for Despina.

CHERRY: Who's she?

ROY: The maid.

CHERRY: But I want a large role.

ROY: It's practically the largest. Every audience takes Despina to their bosom.

DOUG: Bit like the men's wards have already done.

CHERRY: One more crack –

ROY: And, of course, the others pick themselves. Julie as Fiordiligi, Dorabella is Ruth. Doug, you'll be Ferrando and I'll be Guglielmo. Typecasting, really.

LEWIS: Roy –

ROY: We must get started on the costumes. I've told occupational therapy to stop making those baskets –

LEWIS: Roy –

ROY: And the set, my god, who'll paint the backdrops?

LEWIS: [*loudly*] Roy!

[*Everyone stops, even* LEWIS *is surprised at how loudly he yelled. Pause.*]

ROY: Hark! Adolf Hitler has spoken.

[*Almost confidentially to those near him, letting them know he is speaking from experience.*]

All directors are tyrants.

LEWIS: [*more softly*] Roy –

ROY: That's the name.

LEWIS: We've auditioned everyone this morning –

ROY: And you were thorough. Thorough. I was impressed –

LEWIS: And I did notice something –

ROY: Ah, already: details!

LEWIS: No one can sing.

ROY: I can carry a tune, Ruth can –

LEWIS: What I mean is, Roy, no one can sing opera.

[*Pause.*]

ROY: We certainly got up on the wrong side of the bed this morning, didn't we?

LEWIS: Opera voices take years of training.

ROY: Not in the old days. Enthusiasm, natural talent –

LEWIS: And on top of everything else, the opera is in Italian. That's an incredible burden, even for the most brilliant talent. [*A beat.*] Isn't it?

[*Pause.*]

ROY: I aim for the stars, Jerry, is that such a bad thing –

LEWIS: No, I like your enthusiasm –

ROY: Then, let's aim for the stars!

DOUG: [*to* JULIE] I want what Roy's on.

CHERRY: Maybe we should do that play Lewis talked about.

DOUG: It sounded boring.

ROY: I second that.

DOUG: As boring as this opera. Let's do a rock musical. A nude, tribal, let's make love not war, man, rock opera. [*To* CHERRY] You'll stay dressed, of course.

ROY: I've got it! I've licked the problem. Jerry, in his amazing way has hit the nail on the head. Singing and learning Italian is probably a bit too much to ask for, so let's sing it in English. Jerry can translate the Italian into English. We'll start rehearsals immediately.

LEWIS: Roy, I don't think you see my point. It will be hard to go into rehearsals immediately because no one can sing the music.

ROY: Straight to the crux of the problem again! I tell you what, we rehearse it like a proper play, you know, a stage play, then, as we learn the songs, we incorporate them into the stage business we have learnt.

[LEWIS *is beaten by* ROY*'s enthusiasm.* ZAC *collapses head first onto the piano keys with a resounding atonal chord.*]

LEWIS: Is he all right?

ROY: He's broken into the pharmacy again.

DOUG: He's doped to the eyeballs, he'll be fine.

CHERRY: [*looking at* RUTH*'s watch*] Time for lunch.

ROY: The director has to say it.

CHERRY: I'm hungry.

[*Pause. They look to* LEWIS.]

LEWIS: Time for lunch.

CHERRY: Outside, it's beautiful.

ROY: Coming out for a spot of lunch, Jerry?

LEWIS: Might have a look at the translation of the libretto. I'll see how good the English is.

ROY: You're like the best directors, a glutton for work.

[ROY *leaves singing an aria from* Così. *Except for the catatonic* ZAC, *who is still face down on the piano keys and forgotten,* LEWIS *is alone. He sighs, feeling that the whole project is hopeless.*]

LEWIS: [*to himself*] Why can't I ever say no? Just leave. They're mad. It's madness... [*But he knows he won't leave.*]

[*He remembers something. He takes a transistor out of his bag and turns it on. It is his friend,* NICK, *talking about the coming moratorium.* LEWIS *shakes his head as he listens to* NICK *and the interviewer.*]

INTERVIEWER: How many people do you think there will be at the moratorium, Nick?

NICK: Well, Tom, at a rough guess, I'd say twenty thousand.

INTERVIEWER: And for a left wing person like you, what does it mean?

NICK: It means that these people, even the middle class will be radicalised by seeing how many of us are against them. They'll know that to be against the Vietnam war is also to be against the old fossilised government we now have. They'll want the war to end, they'll want changes in our society, they'll want to overthrow the establishment.

[DOUG *enters, overhearing the interview.*]

INTERVIEWER: By overthrow, you don't mean like what happened in Paris, in 1968?

NICK: Barricades and bombs? Why not? Australians, especially young Australians of my age, are getting fed up with our society. We want changes and we want them now!

LEWIS: [*exasperated*] Christ, Nick–!

[*He turns down the volume.*]

DOUG: You think it'll be like that?

[LEWIS *is surprised to see* DOUG, *but recovers quickly.*]

LEWIS: May '68 in Australia? No.

DOUG: Why not?

LEWIS: The French always believe their own rhetoric, Australians are suspicious of rhetoric.

DOUG: That's deep. But it would be good, wouldn't it? Throwing rocks at cops, overturning cars, smashing barricades, burning houses –

LEWIS: [*surprised*] You followed the events of '68?

DOUG: A little. Mum always liked things French. Perfume. Cheese. Frog's legs. She went up the Eiffel Tower on a *Women's Weekly* tour. She thought De Gaulle was as great a President as Churchill. So she was a bit upset when he was nearly overthrown.

[LEWIS *turns off the radio.*]

I'm bothering you.

LEWIS: No, I've heard it all before. Nick's a friend. He has only one problem, he likes the sound of his own voice.

DOUG: Close friend?

LEWIS: Lives with me and my girlfriend.

DOUG: You share her?

LEWIS: [*offended*] No.

DOUG: But you're not married?

LEWIS: No.

DOUG: You believe in free love and that sort of thing?

LEWIS: Free love is a hard concept to define.

DOUG: I believe in free love but it's hard to practise it in here. How close are you to the slaughterhouse?

LEWIS: Next door almost.

DOUG: Smell a lot?

LEWIS: When it's hot.

DOUG: Bet your girlfriend doesn't like it.

[LEWIS *nods his head in agreement.*]

What's her name?

LEWIS: Lucy.

DOUG: In the sky with diamonds. [*He laughs,* LEWIS *smiles.*] Is she pretty, your girlfriend?

LEWIS: Yes.

DOUG: Was Lucy a virgin when you first had her?

[LEWIS *is reluctant to answer.*]

I'm not prying or anything, am I? It's just that in here you miss out on a lot of changes in society's morals. [*A beat.*] So was she a virgin?

LEWIS: No.

DOUG: How many did Lucy have before you?

LEWIS: It's not something I want to talk about.

DOUG: A few, eh? Women like to pretend they don't play around but they're just more secretive about it. They don't brag about it like men.

[*Pause.*]

Going to marry Lucy?

LEWIS: Who knows?

DOUG: Don't. Dad always said to me: you can always find
loneliness in a marriage, but never solitude. [*A beat.*] And I
like my solitude.

CHERRY: [*entering*] Where are the dunnies?

DOUG: Through there. They've got no lights. I hope you'll fall
in but you're too fat.

CHERRY: Go burn a cat.

     [*She goes.*]

LEWIS: Why are they always saying that?

DOUG: It's what I did.

LEWIS: Burn a cat?

DOUG: Cats.

LEWIS: When you were young?

DOUG: No, no, quite recently. It was the fault of the psychiatrist.
I'd been seeing him because of my pyromania – that's a
person who likes lighting fires – but you probably know that
being university educated. You know the problem with
pyromania? It's the only crime where you have to be at the
scene of it to make it a perfect crime, to give yourself full
satisfaction. 'Course, that means the chances of you getting
caught are greater, especially if you're standing in front of
the fire, face full of ecstasy and with a gigantic hard on. So,
the cops got me and I'm sent to a shrink. He tells me that
I've got an unresolved problem with my mother. I think,
hello, he's not going to tell me to do something Oedipal, like
fuck her or something . . . but that wasn't the problem. My
ego had taken a severe battering from her. He said I had
better resolve it, stop her treating me like I was still a child.
It made some sort of cosmic sense. I had to stand up to her.
So I thought about it and realised I had to treat it like a
boxing match, get the first punch in, so to speak, to give me
the upper hand in our relationship. She had five cats. One
night I rounded them up, put them in a cage, doused them
with petrol and put a match to them. Then I opened the cage
door and let them loose. Well, boy, oh, boy, what a racket!
They were running around the backyard burning and howling

– there's no such thing as grace under pressure for a burning cat, let me tell you. I hid in the shrubs when mum came outside to see what was happening. Totally freaked out, she did. Five of them, running around the backyard like mobile bonfires. I figured I'd wait a couple of hours till the cats were dead and mum was feeling a bit sorry for herself and I'd knock on the front door and say to her 'Hi, mum, I've come to talk about our unresolved conflicts' but, oh, no, one of those cats ran into the house. In a couple of minutes the whole bloody house was alight and within half an hour there was no bloody front door to knock on. [*A beat.*] If it wasn't for that damn cat, I wouldn't be here.

CHERRY: [*entering*] It stinks in there, you been in there before me?

DOUG: No, I haven't, but I'll use it now you've warmed up the seat.

   [*He goes.*]

CHERRY: I know why you're in here, you've got nothing to eat.

LEWIS: No, it's fine.

CHERRY: No, it isn't. I'll go and get my sandwiches so I can share them with you.

LEWIS: It's all right, I'll just look at the translation.

CHERRY: I won't talk. I'll eat and watch you work. I like watching people work.

   [*She goes.* ZAC *lifts up his head and looks around. Only* LEWIS *is there.*]

ZAC: Is it time to go?

LEWIS: The others are outside having lunch.

ZAC: Oh. [*A beat.*] Why?

LEWIS: Why?

ZAC: Why is everything ringing?

LEWIS: Are you all right?

ZAC: Can't hear you. [*His face crashes down on the keys again.*]

CHERRY: [*entering with food*] This is the best part, isn't it? Not having to eat lunch in a ward. But in a theatre! [*Giving a*

*sandwich to the reluctant* LEWIS.] Go on, you're too skinny.
[*He takes it and eats slowly.*] So the maid is a big part?
LEWIS: Oh, yes, she gets to pretend to be a doctor, a priest –
CHERRY: Something to extend my acting range? Will outsiders
see the show?
LEWIS: People from outside the institution? Don't know.
CHERRY: If it's going to be a large role then I'll invite my dad.
He'll be surprised to see me out of water. Dad was a great
duck hunter. But we were poor and couldn't afford a dog. He
used me to point and fetch the ducks. Those lakes can get
cold when you're swimming in them with a dead duck in
your mouth. [LEWIS *is astonished by the story. She laughs.*]
Just pulling your leg. Sucked you right in, didn't I? [*A beat.*]
You know, I really like you.
   [ZAC *stands up, slamming the keys, then to no one in
   particular he yells out.*]
ZAC: All right, I'll get The Electric Prunes album!
   [*He storms out, much to* LEWIS's *astonishment, but*
   CHERRY *is used to this type of behaviour. As he goes* ZAC
   *almost runs into* JULIE *who enters and stands nearby, too
   shy to ask* LEWIS *something.*]
LEWIS: [*noticing her*] You want something, Julie?
JULIE: Someone told me you had a transistor.
LEWIS: That one.
JULIE: You're not using it now?
CHERRY: [*to* LEWIS] Eat!
   [*She stuffs a sandwich into his mouth.*]
Get some flesh on your bones.
JULIE: Can I use it? I wouldn't mind listening to some music.
   [LEWIS, *his mouth full, can only nod.*]
Thank you.
   [*She walks out with it.*]
CHERRY: [*whispering to* LEWIS] Typical junkie, needs stimulus
all the time or else her thoughts turn to you-know-what.
   [DOUG *runs in from the toilet, yelling.*]
DOUG: Fire! Fire in the dunnies! Quick! Get help!

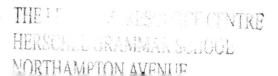
THE ... RESOURCE CENTRE
HERSC... GRAMMA... SCHOOL
NORTHAMPTON AVENUE

[JULIE *and* LEWIS *run off to the toilet.* ROY *and* RUTH *rush in.* DOUG *addresses them.*]

Fire! Fire in the dunnies.

[*They rush into the toilet, then out of the corner of his eye* DOUG *notices* CHERRY *advancing on him.*]

Get a bucket!

[*But she doesn't, instead she throws herself on him, her hands around his throat, choking him.*]

CHERRY: You did it deliberately!

DOUG: [*hoarsely to* HENRY *who has just entered*] Henry...

[*But* HENRY *rushes to the toilets.*]

ROY: [*off*] Buckets!

CHERRY: I'm going to kill you!

LEWIS: [*off*] A hose, I'll get a hose.

ROY: [*off*] Quick!

[CHERRY *pays no attention to the fire but is intent on throttling* DOUG.]

CHERRY: I'm going to kill you for this!


## SCENE THREE

*The theatre.* JUSTIN *is looking at the toilets while* LEWIS *waits for him apprehensively.* ZAC *is at the piano. The others sit around watching* LEWIS *or like* ROY *and* HENRY *study their scripts.* DOUG *is pretending to study his script but is watching* LEWIS *carefully.* JUSTIN *enters from the toilets, grimfaced.*

JUSTIN: Well, that's it, then!

[LEWIS *is glum,* CHERRY *despondent, but* ROY *is elated.*]

ROY: We'll get a new director then. Thank God!

JUSTIN: No, nothing. The experiment is over.

[ROY *is devastated, as are the others.* JUSTIN *takes* LEWIS *aside.*]

I don't think you're up to it. You understand what I am saying, Lewis? This experiment was to bring them out of their shells, not to allow them to wreak havoc. Now the position of a social worker in an asylum can be precarious. This does not look good for me or for you, does it?

LEWIS: I'm sorry.

JUSTIN: Sorry is such an easy word to say. You don't want greater disasters, do you?

DOUG: [overhearing JUSTIN] It was an accident!

JUSTIN: Doug has a problem.

DOUG: My mother for starters.

LEWIS: It won't happen again.

JUSTIN: All right, everyone back to their wards.

DOUG: [to everyone] Don't blame me, blame my mother.

JUSTIN: Be careful, Doug or you might see the inside of the closed ward again.

CHERRY: [loudly] It was me! It was me! Doug isn't to blame.I dropped a ciggie down the toilet.

JUSTIN: You don't smoke.

CHERRY: Yes, I do.

HENRY: [wanting to tell the truth] Nnnnooo, sheee-
[ROY realises the delicacy of the situation.]

ROY: [hitting HENRY] Shut up, Henry!
[There is a silence. JUSTIN looks at everyone, suspecting that CHERRY is lying. He finally turns to LEWIS for the truth.]

JUSTIN: Is that right?

DOUG: Yeh, they wanted to blame me.

JUSTIN: Is that right?
[A silence, everyone looks to LEWIS.]

LEWIS: That's why she spends so much time in the toilets when she should be at rehearsal. It's where she smokes.
[CHERRY grins, LEWIS has come through.]

CHERRY: I'll try and give the ciggies up.

JUSTIN: I don't know...but if it was an accident...all right, it can continue.
[Everyone is pleased. JUSTIN takes LEWIS aside.]

Just a mention about something else, Lewis. Something
personal. You didn't offer to marry Cherry, did you?

LEWIS: [*shocked*] No.

JUSTIN: Must be pulling my leg again. [*A beat.*] Gave you a bit
of a fright – the fire...

LEWIS: Yes.

JUSTIN: Straight out of university and... well, this is probably the
best education: doing theatre, working with such people. You
couldn't learn this at university. You know why, because it's
about people!

LEWIS: Yes.

JUSTIN: The most important thing is to feel you are in control,
but still at the same time listening. Are you listening, do you
feel you are in control?

LEWIS: Yes.

JUSTIN: You'd make the perfect social worker.

[*To* JULIE] Eager to start the day's rehearsals?

JULIE: Yes.

JUSTIN: Remember what I said and don't forget you're going out
there a nobody and coming back a star

[*He picks up the kerosene heater*] We might put the
kerosene heater outside. There's no point in tempting Doug,
is there? [*Cheerily*] Bye.

[*He leaves with the heater.*]

ROY: Places everyone! We'll start the rehearsal with me!

CHERRY: Lewis has to say it.

LEWIS: First scene.

[RUTH *starts to dole out pills to the cast, much to* LEWIS'
*fascination.*]

ROY:              My Dorabella
                 wouldn't do such a thing.
                 Heaven made her faithful
                 as she is beautiful.

ZAC: Hang on a mo, what about the music?

LEWIS: Remember, Zac, we decided to rehearse the opera as a
play, then gradually include the music when people had
learnt their songs.

[ZAC *tries to cover his surprise at this. It is, for him, a*
*new turn of events.*]

ZAC: I know that. Just because my eyes are closed it doesn't
mean I'm asleep. I meant the overture.

ROY: [*irritated*] On the night.

ZAC: Do you want my suggestions or not?

ROY: No –

LEWIS: Yes.

ZAC: If I play the piano all night, it's going to get boring. I'll
play the piano-accordion in the overture.

ROY: You can't play the piano-accordion in Mozart!

ZAC: No piano-accordion, no piano.

ROY: Get lost then, we'll get another pianist.

ZAC: Where?

LEWIS: [*irritated*] Play the piano-accordion!

ROY: [*to* LEWIS] I thought you were tougher than that. Giving in
straight away does not set a good precedent.

DOUG: If I'm not acting for a while I'll go for a piss.

CHERRY: No, you don't buster. This time you'll succeed in
burning this down.

DOUG: I keep on telling you, it was an accident. I lit a match
because I couldn't find the seat in the dark.

CHERRY: Piss outside.

LEWIS: Stay here, Doug, we're still rehearsing this scene.

DOUG: You believe me that I didn't start this fire deliberately?

LEWIS: [*unsure*] Yes.

ZAC: He's a little light, isn't he, that Mozart?

LEWIS: Light?

ZAC: The overture. No suspense. No atmosphere. [*He hums a*
*bit.*] Sort of fairies down the bottom of the garden, isn't it?
That's why the piano-accordion is the answer. I've got one
back in the ward, bit battered, but it'll be okay. Won't be a
mo.

[*He goes.*]

LEWIS: Let's get on with it.

ROY: Right, right, Jerry. Push us.

LEWIS: From the beginning, Roy. Now, remember, you and your
mate are talking about how your girlfriends are faithful but
Don Alfonso is cynical about this. Henry, would you stand?
[HENRY *stands and* LEWIS *gives the signal for* ROY *to
begin.*]

ROY:                    My Dorabella
                       wouldn't do such a thing –

RUTH: Where's the coffee?

LEWIS: Ruth, we might leave the coffee business for the
moment –

ROY: No, no, she's put her finger on something. Props! There.
[*He rushes to a table and gets some coffee mugs, giving
one to* HENRY *and* DOUG *and keeping one for himself.*]
We're drinking coffee then.

RUTH: But there's none in there.

LEWIS: We might pretend for a moment.

RUTH: I can live with illusion as long as I know it's illusion, but
this coffee is not real, is it?

LEWIS: No, they're pretending.

RUTH: The audience thinks it's real coffee?

LEWIS: If the acting is good enough, yes.

RUTH: An illusion of reality. A real illusion in other words?

LEWIS: Yes.

RUTH: But, as I said before: I can handle something being an
illusion or real but not at the same time.
[LEWIS *is flummoxed.*]

ROY: Ruth?

RUTH: Yes?

ROY: Shut up.

[*To* LEWIS] The theatre is no place for metaphysics.

RUTH: It's about coffee – !

LEWIS: Ruth! We might move on. Until we get real coffee we'll
pretend.

RUTH: [*grumpily*] All right.

LEWIS: Roy.

ROY:            My Dorabella
                wouldn't do such a thing.
                Heaven made her faithful
                as she is beautiful.

DOUG:           My Fiordiligi
                would never betray me.
                I believe her constancy
                is equal to her beauty.

[*They look to* HENRY *as it is his cue.*]

LEWIS: Henry, your lines: 'My hair is grey, so I speak with authority . . .'

[HENRY *refuses to say them. Instead he takes a toy soldier out of his pocket and examines it as if he is not part of the rehearsal.*]

Henry, please . . .

[HENRY *shakes his head.* ROY *falls to his knees and starts banging his head on the floor.*]

ROY: Why! Why am I always let down! Why do people let me down!

LEWIS: Roy, don't do that.

DOUG: Roy, you're hurting the floor.

CHERRY: [*to* JULIE, *who laughs*] Do it yourself lobotomy.

LEWIS: Roy! [ROY *stops.*] Henry, you came along here, so you must want to do *Così Fan Tutte*.

HENRY: [*pointing to* ROY] Hhhhhee made me dddddo it.

ROY: For your own good. Look, Henry, you're a failure, as a human being and as a lawyer. *Così* offers you a chance to do something successful at least once in your dismal life.

LEWIS: Roy, no one is a success or failure.

ROY: Tell that to the failures of this world.

HENRY: Rrrrroy is right.

ROY: Out of the goodness of my heart I have given you a major role and what happened? You let me down. Just as you let your parents and your clients down. God knows how you can live with yourself.

LEWIS: I don't think that approach will help, Roy.

ROY: I've known him for six years, Jerry, but you're the director.

[*He sits down sullenly and leans over to* DOUG.]

Couldn't direct traffic down a one way street.

LEWIS: What we might do, Henry, is to come back to this scene. We'll do as much of the next scene as I've translated and you'll see how it's done.

ROY: [*sarcastically*] Oh, bravo! Masterstroke!

LEWIS: [*ignoring* ROY, *he turns to the women*] We'll do scene two. It's a garden by the seashore.

[*They stand, preparing to read from their scripts.*]

DOUG: Oh, everyone, you'll notice I am going outside to urinate. Does that satisfy you all?

CHERRY: I hope you'll get arrested for indecent exposure only there's probably nothing to expose.

[DOUG *exits.*]

LEWIS: You can sit down, Cherry.

CHERRY: But I'm in scene two.

LEWIS: I've only had time to translate to your entrance.

CHERRY: You'll have it done by tomorrow?

LEWIS: If I have time.

CHERRY: You'll make time, won't you?

LEWIS: Yes. [*To* RUTH *and* JULIE] You're in the garden by the seashore.

RUTH: An illusion again. Patently, we are in a theatre.

LEWIS: An illusion, yes. And you're both gazing at miniatures of your lovers.

RUTH: Miniature what?

LEWIS: Paintings. Tiny ones.

RUTH: Not real ones?

LEWIS: We'll get the real ones later.

RUTH: Another illusion. [LEWIS *nods*] Do you want me to give an illusionary performance too?

ROY: [*half to himself*] Someone strangle her.

LEWIS: What do you mean?

RUTH: We're in an illusion of a garden, carrying an illusion of tiny paintings, so shall I sit down and pretend I am acting?

LEWIS: Ruth, just pretend!

RUTH: You're doing a fine job of messing with my head.

JULIE: Ruth, it'll be fine. Let's act out the words. All right?

> [RUTH *nods*. LEWIS *indicates for* JULIE *to start.*]
> Tell me sister
> if one could ever find
> a sweeter mouth
> or a more noble face.

RUTH: Look, see what fire –

Now, am I pretending to be looking at the miniature of my lover here? [LEWIS *nods grimly.*] I just wanted to be certain.

> See what fire is in his eye.

JULIE: This is the face
> of a soldier and a lover.

LEWIS: You can walk if you like. Like you're strolling in the garden, staring at the miniatures, talking about them.

RUTH: What if we trip?

LEWIS: All the rocks are an illusion, so you won't.

RUTH: Of course.

> This is the face
> both charming and dangerous.

LEWIS: Why aren't you strolling, Ruth?

RUTH: I was wondering where you wanted me to walk and how many steps?

LEWIS: Where ever you want to walk and as many steps as you like. Just try to make it natural.

RUTH: Real?

LEWIS: No, natural, like anyone walking. Yes, yes, like in real life. If you walk and talk, as you would in real life, then the steps and the direction will take care of themselves.

ROY: No, it won't Jerry. Direction means to direct. You direct an actor somewhere. Ruth has a good point. I must also point out that in my theatre days the director would come in and block out the whole play in the morning and over the next couple of weeks we'd fill in the emotion and gestures. That's what you want, isn't it, Ruth? I'm not trying to teach you to suck eggs, Jerry, but that woman is crying out for direction.

RUTH: [*to* LEWIS] How many steps do you want me to take?

[LEWIS *feels like giving in but grits his teeth and continues.*]

LEWIS: Walk to that spot there and count the steps.

RUTH: [*walking to the spot*] One, two, three, four, five, six. Six.

LEWIS: It'll be six steps then.

RUTH: Large or small? Because, if it's small, then it could be up to ten, maybe eleven.

[LEWIS *holds his head in his hands.* ZAC *comes in wearing a battered and dusty piano-accordion.*]

ZAC: She's a real beauty. A bit dusty.

ROY: We are trying to rehearse!

ZAC: The music's just as important.

[ZAC *starts to play a tune.*]

ROY: That's not Mozart.

ZAC: Of course not. It's Wagner.

ROY: I hate to point this out, but we're doing *Così Fan Tutte*.

ZAC: Such a pissy opera. Wagner – he's got balls.

ROY: Get out! Get out!

LEWIS: Roy, calm down.

[*He turns to* ZAC.]

He's right, we are doing Mozart.

ZAC: I'm prepared to play the pissy score for the whole opera, only if I do the overture my way, or else it's exit the pianist.

LEWIS: [*to* ROY] Seems fair enough, after all, it's only the overture.

ROY: Someone's just brought a dinner gong to the music of the spheres.

LEWIS: [*taking him aside*] People really don't listen to overtures. They're too busy finding their seats, coughing, opening up their lollies.

ROY: Yes, yes. I'm going to have a word with his doctor though, I think his Lithium should be upped.

[*To* ZAC, *magnanimously*] You can play the Wagner.

[RUTH *is doing her steps.*]

RUTH: I can make it nine, ten or eleven. If I took really big steps I could make it five.

[LEWIS *has had enough.*]

LEWIS: A break! Let's take a break.

ROY: Is it time for one?

LEWIS: Yes.

ROY: Well, you're the boss.

[*People head outside.*]

DOUG: [*to* ROY] I hear the boys of D ward have taken up another petition to try to get rid of you.

ROY: The boys of D ward... what a bunch of whackers.

[ZAC *begins to practise Wagner's 'The Ride of the Valkyries', humming loudly along with it.* LEWIS *slumps in a chair, exhausted.*]

LEWIS: I wonder, Zac, if you could practise outside?

ZAC: Sure.

[*A beat.*] How do you want me dressed? Tux? Perry Como cardigan?

LEWIS: Anything. Anything you like.

[ZAC *is pleased and heads outside, still playing. He stops when he hears a noise. He goes over to the wall and listens closely.*]

ZAC: Sounds like Doug is pissing against the outside wall. Maybe he doesn't like your direction, Lewis?

[LEWIS *smiles and* ZAC, *returning to his playing, heads outside. The hall is quiet now.* LEWIS, *thinking he is alone, takes out a student newspaper and begins to read it when he suddenly notices* JULIE *has remained in the room.* JULIE*'s mood swings wildly as she seems preoccupied with something.*]

LEWIS: Thought you'd gone outside. You seem a bit preoccupied.

JULIE: Bit over the shop today. I had to go and see one of the shrinks. They don't know how to deal with drug users. He called it a 'crutch', I said it was a 'rocket to the stars'. Needless to say, we didn't get on. I'm surprised to see you here. I thought you wouldn't come back. [*A beat.*] They still scare you?

LEWIS: It's not so bad. My grandmother went mad. I went once to the asylum to see her. In her mind she was living in the year before I was born. She thought I was Eric, my father. And he had just married mum and she was about to have me.

JULIE: You pretended to be your father about to father yourself?

[*He nods; both are amused*]

Don't ever tell a psychiatrist that story, they'd have a heart attack on the symbolism of it all.

[*They both laugh.*]

In a way you're sort of testing yourself by coming here?

LEWIS: I guess so. I liked my grandmother, I knew she had gone mad, but she was still my grandmother.

JULIE: It must be strange to be doing plays with amateurs like us?

LEWIS: All I've done is act a bit at university and did some direction. My friend, Nick, is the one who knows all about theatre, only he's more interested in politics. He says politics is the real theatre.

JULIE: He shares a house with your girlfriend, Lucy. Doug has told the whole hospital everything about you.

[*Noticing the newspaper.*]

You're a radical?

LEWIS: [*amused*] Lucy would never call me that. She and Nick edit the newspaper. It's a special edition publicising the moratorium march against the war.

JULIE: [*looking at second page*] Lucy White... that's her?

LEWIS: Yes.

JULIE: Uses a nice shampoo in her hair. Earnest. Serious. Not many jokes? [*He shakes his head, bemused.*] A laugh is as good as a fuck, they say. You two are into free love?

LEWIS: Doug said that?

JULIE: Spread it all over the asylum.

LEWIS: Lucy's not into marriage –

JULIE: You are?

LEWIS: We sometimes talk about commitment –

JULIE: [*amused*] Fidelity, like in *Così*?

LEWIS: But it never gets far.

JULIE: She's not into it?

LEWIS: She's into politics. She hates talk about love. She thinks its icky. 'Love is the last gasp of bourgeois romanticism' she says. She hates me doing an opera about love and fidelity while thousands of Vietnamese are being killed by American troops.

JULIE: Does she play around?

LEWIS: [*laughing*] No.

JULIE: You trust her?

LEWIS: [*uncertainly*] Yes.

JULIE: Do you trust men not to play around?

LEWIS: Men are –

JULIE: Flesh and blood. Women are flesh and blood too – that's what the opera says, doesn't it? Am I irritating you?

LEWIS: I was wondering what you were getting at.

JULIE: I don't like men's double standards, I guess. Men want women to deceive them because it'll prove their worst thoughts about women – and they have a lot of bad thoughts about women. And then they become so righteous, like Guglielmo and Ferrando. I would love to hit up right now. You know what a psychiatrist is? A Peeping Tom with a fancy title. [*She laughs.*] I don't sit in the rec room watching television, I read this stupid libretto, trying to remember the lines. [*They both laugh.*] It's so wonderfully silly. [*Referring to the newspaper photograph*] She's very pretty, but should change her hairstyle. It makes her look like a coffee shop folk singer.

[LEWIS *doesn't know how to take the comment, which is fine by* JULIE. CHERRY *enters, bringing him a cake. She stuffs the cake in his mouth before he is even aware that she is there.*]

CHERRY: Surprise! Fairy cakes. My family brought them in for me. Yummy.

JULIE: Can I read the newspaper?

[LEWIS *can only nod.* JULIE *goes outside with it. Pause.*]

CHERRY: I'm not bothering you, am I?

[*He shakes his head.*]

Just between you and me, I've got a flick knife. If Doug attempts any more arson, then he's a goner. [*Cheerfully she changes to another topic.*] I was looking at the first scene, seeing I had nothing to do, which was totally unexpected after all this talk about how large my part was going to be, when I read the words that Henry says: 'Woman's constancy is like the Phoenix of Arabia. Everyone swears it exists but no one has seen it.' By the way, I think your translation is wonderful. Do you believe women are like that? That they aren't true and faithful? I am. With someone like you I could be true and faithful.

[LEWIS *almost chokes on his fairy cake.* CHERRY *slaps him heartily on the back.*]

Go down the wrong way, did it?

[*She sniffs the air.*]

What is that smell?

[LEWIS *smells it too.*]

Kerosene...

LEWIS: [*realising*] Doug!

[*There is a whoosh! as the kerosene explodes in flames outside.*]

DOUG: [*from outside, exhilarated*] It's burning like a beauty! Someone get me a cat.

LEWIS: [*jumping up*] Not again! [*Running outside, shouting*] Get some buckets!

[CHERRY *is livid. She takes out her flick knife and flicks it open. Its blade is ready for action.*]

CHERRY: If there is anything worse than the wrath of God, its the Wrath of Cherry.

[*She goes outside with great purpose.*]

## SCENE FOUR

*The theatre.* ROY *is depressed.* LEWIS *is at a loss.*

ROY: I need some uppers.

[*Pause.*]

LEWIS: The thing is, Roy, it was always going to be a hard project to do and now that Doug is in the closed ward –

ROY: Put in by you-know-who.

LEWIS: He set fire to this place.

ROY: I thought you people were into 'doing your own thing', but when somebody else does it – Oh, no, shove him straight into C ward.

LEWIS: We could have died.

ROY: But we didn't.

LEWIS: He wasn't taking his pills.

ROY: I need some right now. [*A beat.*] It's not the fact that you've let me down, Jerry, it's more the fact that you've let everyone down. [*He looks at the theatre*] This theatre could have been ringing with the music of the spheres, instead of that, a dreadful silence has descended upon us. I should have done it myself. I knew it from the first time I saw you.

LEWIS: It's not my fault.

ROY: Oh, I get it; if the production had been a success it was all because of you. If it had flopped, it wasn't your fault. How very, very directorial. Like Hitler, 'Oh, my God, you mean to tell me we're fighting on the Russian front and we're losing? Why didn't someone tell me we had three million troops in Russia?' But I won't go on, you'll probably put me in a closed ward.

[JULIE *enters.*]

Don't criticise Mussolini here, or it's the closed ward for you.

[ROY *goes and sits at the back of the stage grumpily imagining the triumphs that might have been.*]

LEWIS: [*to* JULIE] I don't know if you've heard, but without Doug we can't do *Così*. No one else will volunteer for it.

JULIE: I heard. No one in Roy's ward will volunteer because they say they get enough of him as it is.

ROY: [*overhearing*] It's only their sense of humour, you pathetic junkie.

JULIE: [*paying no attention to* ROY] I thought you might want to put on something else.

LEWIS: I have an idea.

ROY: Oh, really, what is it? 'Pussies on heat'?

[LEWIS *and* JULIE *pay no attention to him.*]

JULIE: I'm glad. I like doing theatre, even though it's my first time.

LEWIS: Really? I didn't think you liked what we were doing.

ROY: Give her a poke and get it over and done with, that's what directors do.

[JULIE *and* LEWIS *find themselves, almost automatically, moving out of* ROY'*s hearing. He yells after them.*]

If you poke the director, you'll get the best role.

[*To himself*] Couldn't direct a nymphomaniac to a stag night.

JULIE: I like it because I'm doing something. Using up energy. Getting out of my ward. God, how I hate that ward.

LEWIS: You don't like it here?

JULIE: [*laughing*] What gave you that idea? My parents had me committed. They think it's sort of like a holiday. Those dirty white and olive walls give me the heebie jeebies, they really do. *Così* gave me something to think about, something to do. [*She laughs*] See, I'm happy coming to this burnt out theatre. [*Pause.*]

Doug... It's peculiar about drugs. Doug hates them because he likes to be naturally high all the time. Zac likes them because everything passes like he's in a dream or limbo. I think I'm a naturally addictive personality. I like what they give you here, because not to be on drugs, whatever sort, is like being in limbo for me. Drugs make me feel sort of living. Completely the opposite for Doug. Especially junk. Ever had it? No, you haven't, I can tell. A bit of pot, touch of acid, right?

LEWIS: What's it like?

JULIE: Junk? Like lying in a warm, cloudy river. Some people can't imagine life without love, well I can't imagine life without junk. I know it's stupid, that's why I like doing this theatre thing. Doesn't make me sit in my ward thinking, what I need right now is . . . I'm really full of beans, you know? I could cut your hair in a minute flat.

[LEWIS *laughs.*]

ROY: [*yelling over at them*] So, what's the new play, a one woman monologue?

[*They pay no attention to him.*]

JULIE: I could, you know. That's my profession. Hairdresser. I'd do a good job on you now because I'm not on junk. On junk . . . holy, holy Moses . . . [*She laughs.*] You know, just before I came here, a woman was in my salon for a trim. Just a little bit off here and there. I'd just shot up. Beautiful stuff. Felt like mercury, no finger could hold me down. I had the nods. Everything became real slow. Like time standing still. Each hair required absolute concentration. Hour after hour I devoted myself to that hair and twelve hours later that woman was still there, minus a few curls, if that. She hadn't moved. Too scared that I was going to snip everything except her hair. [*She laughs.*] I should have charged by the hour.

[CHERRY *and* RUTH *enter.*]

CHERRY: The stars are here.

ROY: You're not the stars, the one he's poking is the star.

[LEWIS *is angry with* ROY *but says nothing.* CHERRY *is annoyed to see* JULIE *with* LEWIS.]

LEWIS: You heard about Doug?

CHERRY: He blames you for everything. Apparently he keeps on
   saying over and over 'Once I get out of C ward I'm going to
   kill that bastard'.
   [LEWIS *gives a nervous laugh.*]
   And he will too.
ROY: Look on the bright side, Jerry. For killing an actor he'd
   get life, for killing a director he'd get eternal gratitude.
CHERRY: [*handing her flick-knife to* LEWIS] If he escapes and
   comes after you, have this for protection.
LEWIS: [*giving it back*] Put it away, Cherry, I don't need it.
CHERRY: [*putting it back in her handbag*] It's your funeral.
LEWIS: [*to everyone*] What's happening is this – I can't get
   anyone to play Doug's role, so we'll have to do another play.
RUTH: Can't.
LEWIS: Why not?
RUTH: Learnt my lines. I'm word perfect. Go on, test me.
LEWIS: I'm sure you are.
RUTH: You don't believe me?
LEWIS: I do.
RUTH: No, you don't. I can tell.
LEWIS: Ruth, I've got other things on my mind –
RUTH: Any place, anytime. I know what I'm doing and everyone
   else. Test me. The scene where the two men are leaving and
   we think they're going to war. Julie and I say 'Alas, what do
   I hear?' They're going,' she says. Henry says 'At once.' And
   I go [*taking three steps, to herself*] One, two, three . . . 'Is
   there any way of stopping them?'
LEWIS: That's fine, Ruth, I never doubted you –
RUTH: [*continuing*] And Henry says – if we can get him to talk
   – 'None'. Maybe he can shake his head. Once, twice. How
   many times do people shake their heads for a no answer?
LEWIS: Ruth, that's wonderful, but –
RUTH: Three.
   [*She shakes her head three times.*]
ROY: [*to* CHERRY] He's testy because he didn't get a poke!

RUTH: Then Julie says 'Not a single farewell', and Henry says a few lines, while I . . . [*she takes five steps*] One, two, three, four, five –

LEWIS: [*loudly*] Ruth!

ROY: Someone give him a poke!

RUTH: And I turn and say, 'Where are they?'

LEWIS: [*exasperated*] Ruth, please.

ROY: He's as tense as a ram waiting to be put in the ewe paddock.

LEWIS: [*calming himself*] Sorry, Ruth, I'm a bit tense. Losing Doug has thrown things a bit haywire.

RUTH: Even though I can do it, you hate me.

LEWIS: I don't.

ROY: [*to* RUTH] A workman always blames his tool.

LEWIS: Roy!

ROY: Get the ewe!

LEWIS: All right, let's all calm down.

ROY: Said the captain to the passengers of the Titanic.

LEWIS: Roy, please –

CHERRY: Is the other play you want us to do that religious play?

LEWIS: Religious?

CHERRY: *The Exceptional Ruler.*

LEWIS: It's by a German playwright and it's called *The Exception* –

[ROY'*s face is illuminated by a brilliant idea, or so he thinks.*]

ROY: Oh, my god. My god! [*Everyone looks at him.*] I've got it. [*He looks ecstatic.*] Roy, you done it again. Sometimes I'm so . . . what's the word –

CHERRY: Mentally ill.

[ROY *is so locked into his train of thought that he is not stopping for passengers.*]

ROY: Perspicacious. It was there, before my eyes. [*Pointing to* LEWIS] You! You'll play Ferrando! [LEWIS *is astonished.*] Solved. The show lives. *Così* lives!

[HENRY *enters quietly.*]

LEWIS: Roy, I can't sing.

ROY: So what, neither can the others, but by the time we open you'll be singing like a bird.

LEWIS: But I'm directing the show.

ROY: To be perfectly frank, Jerry, what you've done up until now, no one would call directing. Henry, meet the new Ferrando. [*A beat.*] We'll start rehearsals in five minutes. Nature calls.

[*He goes out.*]

[LEWIS *sits down, stunned, trying to take it all in.*]

JULIE: I'm pleased, I like *Così.* Do we need Zac?

LEWIS: Probably.

CHERRY: Can't. He's having shock treatment. Been a bit depressed lately.

[CHERRY *gives* LEWIS *a sandwich, whispering so* JULIE *won't hear.*]

Here, this will prepare you. It'll be good, won't it, us two on stage together?

LEWIS: I really don't feel hungry.

CHERRY: Yes, you do. [*He takes it obediently.*] Never get involved with a junkie, Lewis, all she wants is money to buy drugs. You know she's porked every psychiatrist in the hospital to get prescriptions for drugs. She's notorious for giving head to them, that's why she's called the head shrinker.

[*As* RUTH *and* HENRY *share a thermos of tea,* NICK *arrives warily;* LEWIS *spots him, pleased to see him.*]

LEWIS: Excuse me, Cherry.

[*He hurries over to* NICK *and they speak without being overheard.*]

Nick, I was expecting you earlier.

NICK: There's a lot of organisation required in setting up a moratorium. You said you were going to help out.

LEWIS: I'm really busy on this.

NICK: A fuckin' Mozart opera. Lucy can't believe it either. I mean, I directed you in two of Brecht's plays, didn't you learn anything?

LEWIS: They want to do it.

NICK: Only mad people in this day and age would do a work about love and infidelity. They're definitely mad.

[*Softly singing*] They're coming to take me away, ha, ha, to the funny farm—

LEWIS: Nick, they'll hear you.

NICK: I'm only doing this as a favour, so you'll help me out on the moratorium committee.

LEWIS: There's been some new developments. I thought I could swing them to do *The Exception and the Rule*, but they still want to do *Così*.

NICK: Christ, you'll never be a director until you can convince them that what you want to do is what they want to do. Okay, let's see what they've got. [*Spotting* JULIE] Wow, she's not half bad.

[*They approach the others as* ROY *enters.*]

ROY: You've got someone to play Ferrando?

LEWIS: No.

[*To everyone*] This is my friend, Nick. We did university productions together. He's a director. I've asked him to come along today to have a look at what we've been doing and give us his opinion.

ROY: You direct?

NICK: Yes.

ROY: You any good?

LEWIS: He's very good.

ROY: Is Jerry any good?

NICK: Jerry?

LEWIS: [*to* NICK] He's Dean Martin, I'm Jerry Lewis.

NICK: [*making a joke about it*] As an actor he's awful, but I make him look good.

ROY: Just the director we need.

NICK: I'll sit over here and watch.

[*To* LEWIS] Do anything you like.

LEWIS: From today I'm also in the play –

ROY: [*to* NICK] We were desperate –

LEWIS: So it's my first attempt at the part –

ROY: Don't worry, Nick will make you look good.

LEWIS: Why don't we take it from the scene where the men have left, pretending to go to war, and Fiordiligi and Dorabella are talking to Despina about how much they'll miss their lovers. Say from 'Ah, without my Guglielmo', Julie.

JULIE:          Ah, without my Guglielmo
                I think I'll die.

RUTH:           Without my Ferrando
                I think I'll bury myself.

CHERRY:         You might think that no woman
                ever died for love.
                Died for a man? Why?
                There's a lot more where they came from.

RUTH:           Do you believe anyone could
                ever love another man
                if she had Guglielmo and Ferrando as a
                    lover?

CHERRY:         Certainly.
                Think about enjoying yourselves.

JULIE:          Enjoying ourselves?

CHERRY:         Enjoy yourselves.
                Take lovers.
                Your gentlemen will be away
                fighting in a war.

RUTH:           Don't insult those pure men.
                They're models of fidelity and perfect love.

CHERRY:         Don't talk nonsense.

    [*She is about to begin her speech when* NICK *jumps up.*]

NICK: Let's stop it there.

CHERRY: I've got my speech.

ROY: Aria!

CHERRY: When I sing it, I'll call it an aria.

NICK: [*to* LEWIS] Mind if I say a few things?

LEWIS: Go right ahead.

NICK: [*to the women*] You've got to move. You're standing there like statues. Where's your motivation? Your emotions?

ROY: [*elated*] Finally – a director!

NICK: [*pointing to* CHERRY] Here's this woman telling you to go out and fuck any men you can –

[*There is a shocked intake of breath from everyone at the four letter word.*]

And you want to remain true to your lovers. It's an old fashioned concept, granted.

[*To* RUTH] But you have to be really pissed off when Despina says there's more where they came from.

[*To* JULIE] What's your name?

JULIE: Julie.

[NICK *grabs her by the shoulders, speaking intensely and intimately to her, using all his charm.*]

NICK: You're doing really well, Julie, but it has to be a little realer when you say 'Without my –' what's his name? Gug–

JULIE: Guglielmo –

NICK: Without my Guglielmo, I'd cark it. [*A beat.*] Now, the old girl is so cynical that you girls, although protesting your love and the men's love for you, move away, while she is almost whispering in your ears, like some tempter, like the very devil himself.

ROY: Brilliant! Couldn't have put it better myself. Are you listening, Jerry?

[LEWIS *nods his head reluctantly.*]

NICK: Okay, let's do it again.

RUTH: Should I take six or seven steps?

NICK: What do you think?

RUTH: Seven.

NICK: Seven it is.

[LEWIS *is astounded that she agreed so quickly.*]

ROY: [*to* LEWIS] He's brilliant, isn't he?

NICK: From the beginning.

JULIE:                     Without my Guglielmo
                          I think I'll die.

RUTH:                     Without my Ferrando
                          I think I'll bury myself.

NICK: Good, good, keep on going –

CHERRY:                   You might think that no woman
                          ever died for love.
                          Die for a man? Why?
                          there's a lot more where he came from.

RUTH:                     Do you believe anyone could
                          ever love another man
                          if she had Guglielmo or Ferrando as her
                               lover?

CHERRY:                   Certainly.
                          Enjoy yourselves,
                          take lovers
                          your men will be away
                          fighting in a war.

RUTH:                     Don't insult those pure men
                          They're models of fidelity and perfect love.

CHERRY:                   Don't talk nonsense.

        [*Pause.*]

     Will I do my speech?

NICK: Go for it.

CHERRY:                   You look for fidelity in a man
                          fidelity in soldiers?
                          Don't make me laugh.
                          They have as much resolve as water.
                          Their tricks are all the same.
                          Lies, deceptions, crocodile tears.
                          All they want is to get into your pants.
                          Once they've got their pleasure
                          they despise us
                          and turn their backs on us.
                          They become tyrants –

and don't expect mercy from tyrants.

We women should pay them back in kind.

[*Pause.*]

[*To* LEWIS] I don't agree with what Despina is saying, of course.

[*The women's performances have been so much better and quicker as everyone realises, including the women.*]

ROY: [*ecstatic*] Brilliant!

[*To* NICK.] So that's how a real director works his magic.

[LEWIS *is irritated.*]

Are you watching this, Jerry?

NICK: We'll go on with the rest of the scene.

LEWIS: It's the end of the scene.

NICK: [*taking script*] What's the next one?

LEWIS: Don Alfonso introduces the two lovers who haven't really gone off to war but return in disguise.

[NICK *looks puzzled, not knowing the story very well, something that has never stopped a director before, and will not stop* NICK.]

They're taking Don Alfonso's bet that their women won't be seduced by them and prove their fidelity.

ROY: Nick, sorry to interrupt here.

[LEWIS *is astonished by* ROY'*s servility towards* NICK.]

NICK: That's all right.

ROY: There's six of us, right? And there's supposed to be hundreds of chorus members off-stage, crowds, troops: all going off to war in ships.

NICK: Off-stage? Easy. Play a record of the opera at this section and put it through the amps. It's off-stage, no one will know the difference and they'll think you've got hundreds backstage.

[NICK *returns to reading the script.*]

ROY: Brilliant! Everything is coming alive. Everything matches my vision.

CHERRY: [*noticing* LEWIS'*s irritation*] Don't cream your pants, Roy.

ROY: No more sleepless nights wondering who can replace Jerry.

CHERRY: He gets like this when he goes off medication.

NICK: What's this?

LEWIS: What's what?

NICK: The lovers are disguised as Albanians.

LEWIS: Yes. I thought I'd put them in contemporary Albanian uniforms.

NICK: Contemporary?

LEWIS: They're the easiest. They have no ranks or colours on them.

NICK: But they're communist.

LEWIS: That's half the joke.

NICK: Half the joke? A bit of a kick in the face of a poor nation struggling to feed its people, isn't it? Here we are, supporting the Viet Cong and you're laughing at their supporters, the Albanians.

ROY: Jerry, do whatever Nick says.

LEWIS: Hang on, Roy.

[HENRY, *who has become progressively agitated, thumps the piano. Anger repairs most of his stutter.*]

HENRY: [*pointing to* NICK] You sssssupport the cccommunists?

NICK: Yes.

HENRY: In Vietnam?

NICK: Sure.

HENRY: You give money to North Vietnam?

NICK: For medical supplies.

HENRY: To the enemy?

NICK: Yeh.

HENRY: [*banging chair on the floor*] Traitors! Traitors! Traitors!

NICK: [*to* LEWIS] You'd better get some nurses.

[*But it is too late.* HENRY *rushes at him and grabs him in a bear hug.*]

Now, hang on here.

HENRY: You're a traitor.

ROY: Henry, drop him, that's your director.

NICK: [*to* LEWIS] Get the nurses!

[HENRY *does not let go of* NICK. *He turns to* LEWIS.]

HENRY: You are a communist too?

LEWIS: No.

HENRY: But you support the Viet Cong against us?

LEWIS: Against American imperialism? Of course.

[HENRY *throws* NICK *down,* ROY *rushes to his aid.*]

ROY: Are you all right, Nick? Cut his part, that'll teach him a
lesson.

CHERRY: [*to* RUTH] What's this about Vietnam?

RUTH: It's a place somewhere in Asia. There's a war going on.

CHERRY: You're always the last to know things in an asylum.

[HENRY *takes several toy soldiers out of his pocket and
puts them on the table and points to them.*]

ROY: Put them away, Henry. He's got thousands of them back
in his ward. He's collected toy soldiers for years.

HENRY: My ffffather fought in the war for you. For you and
ffffor me. He was a ggggreat man. You are traitors.

LEWIS: Henry, listen –

NICK: Fuck me dead, Lewis, how do you deal with –

HENRY: Do not swear! I do not work with ttttraitors. Australia
is at war against communists and you . . . you sssstab my
father in the back.

NICK: That's it, I'm not putting up with this right wing crap.

[*He goes to leave.*]

LEWIS: Nick!

NICK: [*to* LEWIS] Not only are they nuts, but they're right wing
nuts.

ROY: [*to* HENRY] If only your family had forced you to do tax
law instead of criminal law you wouldn't be such an
emotional mess.

[NICK *leaves.*]

Nice one, Henry. Nice one, destroying our chance to create
a masterpiece. [*Running after* NICK.] I'll get him back.

[*Silence.*]

LEWIS: Henry, I am not a communist. I do not send money to
North Vietnam for medical supplies. Nick does, I do not. I
am against this war, but I am not supporting the enemy. We
must support any way of getting Australia and America out
of this quagmire.

HENRY: You are a traitor. Australian soldiers die, die, and you
wave fffffffflags for the Viet Cong.

LEWIS: I don't want to see Australian soldiers die, do you?

HENRY: Nnnnnno. My fffffather was a ggggreat soldier. I have
all his medals. He was ffffamous!

LEWIS: We're agreed. We don't want to see Australian soldiers
die in a meaningless war.

HENRY: It is a war with meaning. It is to stop communism.

JULIE: The communists are winning, Henry, we're losing.

HENRY: Wwwwash your mouth.

ROY: [*entering*] Is that how you operated in court, Henry? Hate
to be facing the death penalty with you as my attorney.

HENRY: Shut up!

> [ROY *is stunned to see* HENRY *so aggressive towards him.*
> HENRY *turns to* LEWIS.]

You made fun of us all by making the Alb . . . Al . . .

ROY: Albanians.

> [HENRY *shows his fist to* ROY, *silently threatening to hit
> him if he interrupts again.*]

HENRY: Albanian communists. You make fun of us by making
us communists.

ROY: [*irritated*] I was the one who chose this opera.

HENRY: This *Così* condones the cccorruption of innocence.
Women are told to be tramps. Free love. Women are not to
be trusted.

LEWIS: Henry, it doesn't condone –

HENRY: Be quiet. My mother only llloved my fffather, no one
else. He died in Kkkoreaa and she llloved nnnone else but
me.

> [*There is an embarrassed silence.*]

LEWIS: I wasn't making fun of you by dressing up Guglielmo and Ferrando as Albanian communists. I just thought it was funny, that's all. I thought it was funny that they disguised themselves as communists, seeing it's a world of aristocrats. And the women: that's what the opera's about. Whether love is an unswerving emotion and whether women can remain true. It's a comedy.

HENRY: Whether women can remain true is a ttttragedy.

[*He starts to leave.*]

LEWIS: Henry! Henry!

[LEWIS *jumps in front of him.*]

Henry, I don't want you to leave.

[HENRY *decides to walk around* LEWIS.]

Henry!

[LEWIS *pushes* HENRY *back. He reacts and pushes* LEWIS.]

I'm not going to let you walk out on us! You'll have to hit me to get out.

[HENRY *raises his fist as if to hit* LEWIS, CHERRY *and* RUTH *cry out.*]

Hit me, it's the only way I'm going to allow you to leave us. [*A beat.*] Go on, hit me.

[HENRY *pauses and then drops his arm.*]

HENRY: I don't want to hit you. I like you, you're not the Viet Cong.

[HENRY *walks around* LEWIS.]

LEWIS: Henry. Stop. [HENRY *stops.*] I have an idea. Why don't we make Ferrando and Guglielmo disguise themselves as Australian soldiers?

HENRY: Like my fffffather?

LEWIS: Like your father.

[*Pause.*]

HENRY: All right.

[*Pause.*]

LEWIS: Okay. Let's start from where the two lovers return disguised as Australian soldiers.

ROY: When's Nick coming back?

# ACT TWO

## SCENE ONE

*The theatre. The music from Act One, scene five of* Così Fan Tutte *is played on a gramophone operated by* ROY. HENRY, *who is supposed to be miming to the music, sings loudly. He stands downstage behind a hospital trolley on which is a collection of his toy soldiers and a toy boat. In time with the music – the soldiers and people singing the Number 8 chorus – he marches his toy soldiers on to the boat. Nearby water drips through the hole in the roof. During the song,* RUTH *gets a bucket and puts it under the dripping water.*

CHORUS:          Bella vita militar!
Ogni di si cangia loco
Oggi molto, doman poco
Ora in terra ed or sul mar.
Il fragor di trombe e pifferi
Lo sparar di schioppi e bombe
Forza accresce al braccio e all'anima
Vaga sol di trionfar.
Bella vita militar!

    *[By now all the soldiers are in the boat and he wheels the trolley off.* ROY *stops the music.]*

LEWIS: That's good, Henry, but you don't have to sing to it, you can just mime it.

HENRY: *[slightly aggressively]* I ffffelt like it.

LEWIS: *[not wishing to upset him ]* Fair enough.

ROY: Do you think they'll get the idea that the toy soldiers symbolise real soldiers?

LEWIS: I'm sure.

ROY: You're dealing with a mad audience, you know.

LEWIS: It gives the audience a good indication of what a huge crowd of soldiers are going off to war.

ROY: [*not so sure*] Whatever you say, Jerry.

LEWIS: [*sarcastically*] Thank you, Roy.

> [JULIE *and* CHERRY *enter wearing raincoats.* CHERRY *carrying a bag.*]

ROY: You're late, we had to go back and do the farewell scene again.

JULIE: [*taking off raincoat*] It's pouring out there.

CHERRY: I stopped off at Occupational Therapy to pick up a magnet.

> [*Taking out sandwich and stuffing it in* LEWIS's *mouth.*]

It's a bit wet, I'm afraid. Eat. Go on, you have to put on more weight. They hadn't even started making it.

ROY: What did I tell you? Asylums are the most inefficient places on this earth.

CHERRY: No one knew what a Dr Mesmer magnet looked like. Dr Posner was there and he said he was a carlton.

LEWIS: Charlatan.

CHERRY: And I agreed with him. A Mesmer magnet never helped anyone, it was a fraud.

LEWIS: That's not the point, Cherry. The two men are pretending to be poisoned to try and win over the girls and Despina pretends to be a Mesmerist and helps them recover. It's a satire on Mesmer and his supposed cures.

CHERRY: Whatever. I thought we should make it more real. The women aren't twits, are they? Even though the opera makes them out to be. What if the boys' recovery was really terrible, horrific –

ROY: Now we've got another director!

> [CHERRY *reaches into her bag and takes out equipment for shock treatment.*]

Mozart didn't have that in mind.

LEWIS: What is it?

CHERRY: [*enjoying this.*] Let's show him, Roy.

ROY: Not on your Nellie.

CHERRY: Come on.

ROY: Brings back too many memories.

CHERRY: [*to* LEWIS] It's for shock treatment. Put it on.

> [*She puts on the head strap.*]
>
> Lie on the floor. Go on, it's not attached to the electric current. It won't hurt. Lie down.
>
> [LEWIS *lies on the floor.*]
>
> So here comes Despina.
>
> [*To the other women.*] In position for the scene, girls. Roy, down there.

ROY: No.

LEWIS: Roy, it's acting.

> [ROY *reluctantly lies on the floor.*]

CHERRY: I will also have a fake battery for the electric current.

> [*She puts on* ROY's *head gear.*]
>
> [*To women.*] You are worried – you think I am a doctor –

ROY: [*to* LEWIS] Stop her directing or you'll create a monster –

RUTH: You're Cherry, pretending to be Despina, pretending to be a doctor –

LEWIS: Ruth! Go with the flow.

CHERRY: This is a magnet equipment which the great Doctor Mesmer discovered in Germany and then became famous in all of France. [*A beat.*] I'll shoot a bolt of electricity through you, Roy, so you can show Lewis how to act it.

ROY: I don't want to.

LEWIS: Come on, Roy.

ROY: Mozart is about love, not madness.

CHERRY: Act!

> [*He gives in and she pretends to put bolts of electric currents through* ROY.]
>
> One volt, two volts, three volts.
>
> [ROY *starts to convulse as if real shocks are being sent through him. It looks so real that* JULIE *and* HENRY *are concerned for him and empathise.* CHERRY, *though, is enjoying this.*]

LEWIS: [*becoming concerned*] Are you all right, Roy?

CHERRY: Forty, eighty, a hundred –

LEWIS: Roy!

[*He stops convulsing and smiles triumphantly.*]

ROY: Had you all going there, didn't I? Method acting. Had a lesson in it when I did Rep.

CHERRY: Okay, the both of you.

[*She pretends to put electricity through the both of them.* LEWIS *and* ROY *convulse.*]

Two hundred. Three hundred. Four hundred . . .

[*She snaps her fingers, signalling* RUTH *and* JULIE *to say their lines.* HENRY *joins in at the appropriate moment.*]

| | |
|---|---|
| JULIE: | They're moving. |
| RUTH: | Twisting |
| HENRY: | Sssssshaking. |
| JULIE: | They'll hit their heads. |
| RUTH: | They'll bash their heads. |
| CHERRY: | Hold their heads steady. |
| RUTH and JULIE: | We'll do that. |
| CHERRY: | Hold tight. |
| | Courage. |
| | Now, they're safe from death. |
| JULIE: | They're looking around. |
| RUTH: | They're recovering their strength. |
| HENRY: | The doctor's worth all the gold in Peru. |

[CHERRY *claps her hands to end the demonstration.*]

CHERRY: Much more effective than a Mesmer magnet, isn't it? More theatrical.

LEWIS: We may as well go to the end of the scene.

CHERRY: We did that yesterday, it's all that kissing and stuff. This seems realer, doesn't it?

RUTH: Yes, the more real it is, the more real it is.

ROY: We have a theatre reviewer in our midst.

CHERRY: And it makes me less of a fake and you see why a woman's heart would soften towards a man if she saw what was happening to him in shock treatment.

JULIE: It's supposed to be a comedy.

RUTH: Comedy is better when it's real.

CHERRY: It makes you two seem less foolish.

JULIE: But we are. That's what love is, being foolish.

CHERRY: Lewis?

LEWIS: I suppose you're right. The boys' winning of the girls' hearts should be hard won.

CHERRY: [*triumphantly*] Most women fight hard to keep men out of their pants. You may like being foolish, but most women are not.

JULIE: [*to* LEWIS] I've always thought that love was being foolish and stupid. It's about being on the edge and I like being on the edge. It's not divine madness like some people think, there's no such thing as divine madness, madness is just madness. Love is hallucinating without drugs.

ROY: Love is what you feel when you don't have enough emotion left to hate.

[*His definition stuns everyone.*]

CHERRY: That's an awful thing to say about love.

LEWIS: Why are you keen to do *Così* then?

ROY: It's true. Hate is a much more pure emotion. We choose our enemies with greater care than our lovers. That's why hatred lasts longer. You have enemies for life, but never lovers. Music is what love between humans should be. And we've thrown out the music from this opera.

LEWIS: We just won't have time to learn the music.

RUTH: You should never have got him to do that shock treatment. He's depressed now.

[ZAC *enters, dripping wet, with a cardboard box.*]

ZAC: Enter the genius.

LEWIS: You've finished the set model?

[ZAC *puts it on the table and everyone rushes to it.*]

ROY: [*disappointed*] It's only white walls.

ZAC: Lewis said to keep it simple.

ROY: May as well be back in our wards.

CHERRY: You said you were a painter: there's no garden, no seashore.

ZAC: I was a house painter.

LEWIS: Bit stark, Zac.

ZAC: It's not all of it. I sit at the piano, not playing music day after day, and I think. And last night it came to me, while I was in bed, humming the Electric Prunes *Mass in F minor*, it came to me, a vision, a white light pouring into the ward like Annunciation Light –

ROY: [*half to himself*] Christ, he's been nicking stuff from the pharmacy again.

ZAC: A blinding white light of an idea, a way to solve the problem of creating the world of the garden in the last act. [*Showing them by rearranging the box*] Voila!

LEWIS: I like it.

JULIE: You're a genius, Zac.

ZAC: I know.

JULIE: What are you on?

ZAC: A lower dosage. It's amazing how much more bright the world seems.

RUTH: Are you going to use real trees?

ZAC: I can't stand real things. If I could put up with reality I wouldn't be in here.

[ROY *notices a wet rolled up poster brought in with the box. He unfolds it and is horrified.*]

ROY: What's this?

ZAC: My idea for the poster. Mozart in a strait-jacket.

ROY: My god!

JULIE: Neat, Zac.

ROY: And this name? Who's this person?

ZAC: Da Ponte.

ROY: Who's he? What's his name doing next to Mozart's?

ZAC: He wrote the words.

ROY: What words?

ZAC: *Così Fan Tutte's* words. I thought you knew the opera backwards.

ROY: No one cares who wrote the words. Why do you think an opera has music – so no one will have to pay attention to the words!

LEWIS: But we're speaking the words.

[ROY *is in despair. He walks away. The others turn their attention to the poster.*]

CHERRY: [*horrified*] It's Cherry, not Cheery!

HENRY: Why is my nnnnname so small?

ZAC: I ran out of space.

[CHERRY *takes the poster and takes out a pen.*]

CHERRY: Give me this.

[*She starts to change it.*]

ZAC: Hey!

ROY: And take out that Pontiac fellow's name too!

[LEWIS *goes over to* ROY *who is sitting by himself.*]

LEWIS: What's up, Roy?

ROY: I'm down.

[LEWIS *laughs at the unintended word play but* ROY *is offended.*]

LEWIS: Was it the set? Didn't you like it?

[ROY *shrugs, he doesn't feel talkative.*]

You didn't like doing the shock treatment?

ROY: It's not like the real thing, I suppose.

LEWIS: We can change it back to what Mozart wanted.

ROY: Far be it for me to make suggestions, especially when you allow Cherry to make them.

LEWIS: I want the others to contribute, it makes them feel part of the show.

ROY: So I'm beginning to find out. Democracy is foreign to theatre, Jerry. You and I know that, it's just that you want to pander to the mob.

LEWIS: Some good ideas result.

ROY: Sometimes a vision is destroyed. [*A beat.*] I had a dream, Jerry, and it is fading. There would be music, music of the spheres, colourful costumes, joie de vivre, a world that was as far removed from this depressing asylum as possible. A world that was like my childhood: tea parties, dances in our ballroom, circus performers coming to perform just for me. My mother in Parisian gowns – she flirting with the men, waving her fan so fast, it was a blur – servants dancing on fingertips, French tutors, lullabies goodnight sung to me by my beautiful mother, summer days and lemonade brought to me by a maid as I sat on the front veranda listening to the piano inside playing Mozart. That's the world I wanted *Così Fan Tutte* to capture – recapture. But it's gone, the music too.

LEWIS: I think I have a solution to the music.

ROY: They won't be ready to sing. It's hopeless!

LEWIS: Chin up. I think we can have Mozart's music in a bit of it.

ROY: [*optimistically*] You think so?

LEWIS: Yes. Leave it to me. Okay?

> [ROY *nods in agreement.*]

> [*To others*] Okay, back to work.

CHERRY: [*grumbling*] What about lunch?

LEWIS: [*to everyone*] All right, let's get back to rehearsal. We haven't got much time. We open on Friday.

ROY: We'll never do it.

LEWIS: We will. But we'll also have to rehearse on Friday afternoon.

JULIE: Isn't that the first day of your moratorium?

LEWIS: This comes first.

CHERRY: Good.

LEWIS: We'll go on from where we left off this morning. Ferrando seducing Fiordiligi.

CHERRY: It's easy to see that Fiordiligi's not like Dorabella, who was a bit of a tart giving in so easily. At least one can say that most women aren't like her.

RUTH: It wasn't me, it was the character.

LEWIS: [*enjoying getting back at her*] You were pretending?

RUTH: [*uncomfortable with the admission*] Yes.

HENRY: My wife was like Dorabella.

CHERRY: Didn't even know you were hitched, Henry.

HENRY: She was a tttttemptress.

[*Everyone looks at him amazed. Pause.*]

LEWIS: Okay. Let's take it from your last lines.

[ROY *joins* RUTH, *his depression is lifting.*]

RUTH AND ROY:      Oh, happy exchange
                            of heart and affections
                            what new pleasure
                            what sweet pain.

[*They go off as they would on stage.* LEWIS *looks to* JULIE *and, like Da Ponte's stage direction says, she enters in agitation, followed by* LEWIS *as Ferrando.*]

LEWIS:                 Unkind woman, why are you running from
                            me?

JULIE:                  I've seen a snake, a monster.

LEWIS:                 Now, cruel woman, I understand you.
                            The snake, the monster
                            and all that's fiercest in the Libyan desert
                            You think I'm all of those.

JULIE:                  It's true, you rob me of my peace.

[*Suddenly the lights go out. The theatre is plunged into darkness.*]

CHERRY: Hey!

RUTH: [*unnerved*] It's Doug! It's Doug! Lewis, it's Doug.

LEWIS: It's not, Ruth. Calm down.

ROY: It's probably the fuse box, I'll go and see.

[*He heads off to fix the fuse. Pause.*]

ZAC: Hey, let's have an orgy!

CHERRY: Want a sandwich, Lewis?

LEWIS: No, thanks, Cherry.

CHERRY: Yes, you do.

[*She gets up to go and give him one and accidentally bumps into the table, sending the model onto the floor.*]

ZAC: What was that?

CHERRY: Nothing.

JULIE: I like this. I like the dark. That's what I hate about the wards – they're never really totally dark, there's always a light on in the corridor or whatever. Never true pitch black.

RUTH: I'm not keen on it. I used to have a boyfriend who tied me up and put me in a wardrobe so I wouldn't run away. Four knots or maybe it was three. He'd sit outside the wardrobe door and tell me he'd kill me if I ran away.

JULIE: Did he gag you?

RUTH: No.

LEWIS: [amazed] He still allowed you to talk.

RUTH: He said it was the glue that held our relationship together. He left me when I slashed his car tyres. He said it was the straw that broke the camel's back. I cried for days. He just wanted me for sex. Men like sex more than women because they don't have to clean up the mess.

[CHERRY *has been searching the floor for the sandwich she dropped when she bumped into the table and now, with a sigh of satisfaction, she has found the sandwich and puts it back together in the darkness..*]

CHERRY: Where are you, Lewis?

LEWIS: Over here.

CHERRY: [*putting her foot the in bucket of water catching the drips*] Damn!

LEWIS: What's the matter?

CHERRY: Nothing!

LEWIS: Do you want a hand?

CHERRY: It's like that game you play blindfolded. I used to be good at it when I was young. You guess where people are. [*Bumping into* RUTH] Damn!

RUTH: [concerned] Doug!

CHERRY: It's me. That's strange, I generally have a sixth sense where people are, especially people I like.

HENRY: They dddddeserved it.

LEWIS: Who, Henry?

CHERRY: I hear you, Lewis, am I getting hot?

HENRY: The men in *Così*. Ppppretending to be other people. And look what's happened to them, their ggggirls have fallen for the other ffffriend.

CHERRY: [*a bit more desperately*] Am I hot?

JULIE: What would you do if that happened to you, Lewis?

LEWIS: What?

JULIE: If your friend Nick fell for your girlfriend?

LEWIS: And she fell for him? Feel betrayed, I guess.

CHERRY: [*touching* ZAC] There you are!

ZAC: Get your hands off me, you mad dog.

CHERRY: Am I getting warmer, Lewis? [*Stumbling around in a new direction*] I feel that I am. I know I am, I can feel your body heat.

>   [JULIE *reaches out and touches* LEWIS. *He thinks it's* CHERRY.]

LEWIS: You got me, Cherry.

CHERRY: [*puzzled*] No, I haven't.

>   [JULIE *laughs.*]
>   What's so funny?

JULIE: Nothing. [*Touching* LEWIS' *face*] What would you do, Lewis? Would you hit him? Like Dorabella and Fiordiligi, it's just as easy for a woman to fall in love as it is for a man.

CHERRY: [*desperately*] Am I getting warm, Lewis?

>   [JULIE *giggles,* CHERRY *is suspicious.*]
>   Lewis?

>   [ZAC *walks into* RUTH.]

RUTH: [*yelps*] Doug!

ZAC: It's Zac!

CHERRY: Lewis?

>   [ZAC *takes the opportunity to feel her up.*]

RUTH: [*slapping him*] I don't care who you are – stop it!

CHERRY: What's going on?

RUTH: [*to* ZAC] Touch me again and I'll make you regret it.

>   [ZAC *pays no attention and lifts up her skirt.*]
>   I said – stop it!

[*She whacks him and he falls to the floor.*]

CHERRY: Is that you, Lewis? Lewis, where are you?

[LEWIS *and* JULIE *laugh at what is happening.*]

What are you two doing? I don't want to play any more. Where are you, Lewis? You're pathetically thin, you need to eat.

[JULIE *kisses* LEWIS. *He responds and they kiss passionately. Suddenly the lights come back on. But as their eyes are closed, they don't immediately realise and the others see the kiss vividly.* CHERRY *is horrified and furious.*]

ROY: [*off*] Hey, I did it!

[CHERRY *marches over to* LEWIS *and slams the sandwich into his hand.*]

CHERRY: Eat!

ROY: [*entering*] Master of all trades. Some rain got into the fuse box.

[*Noticing* ZAC's *bloody nose.*]

What happened to you?

ZAC: I fell.

[ROY *notices the broken model on the floor and the bucket no longer catching water.*]

ROY: I leave you lot alone for a moment and chaos reigns. That's what happens when you work with amateurs.

CHERRY: Eat!

[*Embarrassed at being caught out,* LEWIS *eats.*]

ZAC: My model's broken, and I think my nose is too.

CHERRY: [*quietly, to* JULIE] Kiss him again and I'll break your fuckin' arm.


## SCENE TWO

*The theatre. Evening. Lewis has his transistor on and the music is Velvet Underground's 'Candy Says', though he is not*

*listening to it. As he arranges the furniture for rehearsal he*
*speaks some of Ferrando's lines to himself.*

LEWIS:                My Dorabella wouldn't do such a thing
                      Did she misbehave?
                      *[Enthusiatically]* Not that I have any doubts
                      about her.
                      What? Speak out! Did she fall for you?
                      Oh, my God, if I even suspected-
          *[Noticing he needs something]*Broom...
          *[He goes out. A few moments later* LUCY *enters.]*
LUCY: Lewis?
          *[She switches off the transistor, as she does so she notices*
          *the script and reads from it.]*
                      Are you raving?
                      Why would you ruin yourself
                      For a worthless woman?
          *[Throwing the script on a chair]* My god!
          *[*LEWIS *enters with the broom, surprised to see* LUCY*]*
LEWIS: Lucy?
LUCY: I've come to pick you up and take you to the *Galileo*
      rehearsals.
LEWIS: Sorry, I can't.
LUCY: Are you going to let Nick down? What about the
      moratorium meeting?
LEWIS: Can't do that either. I got special permission to rehearse
      *Così* after they've had dinner. We're running out of time.
LUCY: Make a decision, Lewis.
LEWIS: Decision?
LUCY: Between going to the moratorium meeting or staying
      here.
LEWIS: They need me.
LUCY: You can't go to both.
LEWIS: We open soon.
LUCY: Make a choice!
          *[Silence. He thinks.]*

LEWIS: Mozart. I'm not going to let them down.

LUCY: Working with these people has changed you. We used to talk about things. Important things. Now all you can talk about is reactionary drivel like *Così Fan Tutte*.

LEWIS: It's about important things - like love and fidelity.

LUCY: How to understand how capitalism exploits the working class is important. How to stop the war in Vietnam is important. How to make a piece of theatre meaningful and intelligent, like Brecht does, is important. After bread, a shelter, equality, health, procreation, money comes maybe love. Do you think the starving masses give a fuck about love? Love is an emotional indulgence for the privileged few.

LEWIS: Without love the world wouldn't mean much.

LUCY: Lewis, get a grip on yourself. You've always mistaken lust for love. Look at this theatre, a burnt-out wreck. A bloody great hole in the ceiling. An opera with just a piano and performed by mad people. About what? Two wealthy couples worried about fidelity. I'm going to Nick's rehearsals.

LEWIS: You hate the guy. You think he's an egotistical pig.

LUCY: Sure he can grate on people, but he gets things done. He's doing a play that's relevant and he's doing something about the war in Vietnam. After rehearsals we'll go on to the moratorium meeting. It's going to be huge. Absolutely huge. The biggest protest ever seen in Australia.

LEWIS: You're seeing a lot of someone you don't like.

LUCY: He's a fantastic organiser. Without him the committee would be in a shambles.

[*Pause.*]

LEWIS: Are you having an affair with him?

LUCY: You sound like someone out of a farce.

[*Pause.*]

LEWIS: Are you?

[*A beat.*]

LUCY: Of course.

[LEWIS *is stunned.*]

It's only a fling. It doesn't mean anything.

LEWIS: You're sleeping with the both of us?

LUCY: I have sex with him and sleep with you.

LEWIS: What does that mean for us?

LUCY: Lewis - it's not as if we're married.

LEWIS: [*quoting Cosi*] Woman's constancy is like the Arabian Phoenix. Everyone swears it exists, but no one has seen it.

LUCY: Don't quote that fuckin' opera at me! Is that what you think of women?

LEWIS: Well you're not an Arabian Phoenix, are you?

LUCY: No, I'm a woman. Ever heard of a man who is faithful?

LEWIS: Women pretend they're true and faithful --

LUCY: Because that's what men want us to say. That's how they want us to be, even if they're not true and faithful themselves.

[*Pause.*]

LEWIS: It's over. I'm shifting out of the house.

LUCY: Are you sure this is not a French farce? Is someone going to pop out of that door?

[*Someone does. Both are startled to see* DOUG *enter, his face covered in bandages.*]

LEWIS: Doug?

DOUG: What did you expect? The Messiah? [*To* LUCY] Hi.

LEWIS: I thought you were in the closed ward?

DOUG: Snuck out. Thanks for letting Cherry go to work on me with a flick knife.

LEWIS: I had my hands full fighting the fire. Why are you here, Doug?

DOUG: Come to kill you. No, seriously, I wanted to know about *Cosi*. How's it going?

LEWIS: Good.

DOUG: Good? I was wondering because in a closed ward you only get to hear rumours. You took my part?

[LEWIS *nods.*]

Can I have it back now?

LEWIS: Will you please go.

DOUG: You his girlfriend?

> [LUCY *nods.*]

> Great tits.

LUCY: [*to* LEWIS] I have to go now.

DOUG: Do I make you nervous? I have a problem with my social mores. Make love, not war, eh? What I don't understand, Lewis, is that you've been shagging Julie and yet your girlfriend is really attractive. Sensitive too, I bet.

LUCY: Who's this Julie?

DOUG: It's amazing. Every fellow in the hospital wants her but you're the only one she's gone for.

LEWIS: Doug, will you just go.

LUCY: You're screwing a mental patient?

DOUG: I can understand how you feel, Lucy. Julie's a looney and a junkie.

LUCY: The Arabian Phoenix!

LEWIS: I'm not having sex with her.

LUCY: And your holier than thou attitude.

DOUG: I've noticed that too. How do you feel cheating on your girlfriend, Lewis?

LEWIS: I am not! She's cheating on me!

DOUG: I don't believe that.

> [*To* LUCY] Want a root?

LUCY: That's it, I'm going?

> [LUCY *storms out of the hall. Silence.*]

DOUG: Women - they're amazing, eh? Great bum too.

LEWIS: Go burn a cat.

> [*A smiling* ROY *enters.*]

ROY: Evening, thespians!

> [*To* DOUG] The nurses from closed ward are looking for you.

DOUG: Christ...better piss off out the back.

> [DOUG *hurries out.* ROY *notices a glum* LEWIS.]

ROY: Got the glums, Jerry?

> [*He puts his arm around* LEWIS' *shoulder.*]

> Cheer up, old son. It's time for the music of the spheres!

## SCENE THREE

*The theatre. The walls are white. It is opening night.* ZAC *is dressed up as a Bavarian, wearing lederhosen, with a small bandage across the bridge of his nose where* RUTH *hit him. He plays 'The Ride of the Valkyries' on a piano-accordion. It is as if he is opening the real show when, at the end of the piece,* LEWIS *comes on stage wearing the uniform of an Australian soldier.* ZAC *is very zappy.*

ZAC: Well, what do you think?

LEWIS: Maybe it's a bit late to include it.

ZAC: You've never had the time to listen to it.

LEWIS: The show opens in an hour.

ZAC: What about me? Originally I was going to play piano, now all I do is turn on the record player near the end.

LEWIS: Yes, you know the problems about no one being able to sing to the music. Can you put the music on at the right spot?

ZAC: Sure. When Henry starts his aria near the end. Got it. What if I put more zap into the overture –

LEWIS: But you'll remember to put it on?

ZAC: Sure. I purposely didn't take me medication today so I'd be right on top of everything. So we'll go with the overture? It'll put them in the right mood. We open with a piece of toe tapping Wagner to get them in the right mood. Right? I mean, I know the audience, they can be dangerous.

LEWIS: [*against his better judgement*] All right.

ZAC: Now, what do you reckon we finish with the destruction of Valhalla? The boys have revealed themselves, the girls ask forgiveness, they sing about how happy they are and there's the wedding . . . but instead of the insipid happy-go-lucky music of Mozart, there is the Wagner that foreshadows what is going to happen to the couples in the future: a life of torment and adultery.

LEWIS: I don't think Mozart is saying that.

ZAC: I thought that was your concept?

LEWIS: I don't have a concept, I'm a director.

ZAC: I need a piss. First night nerves play havoc with my bladder. Be back in a mo and I'll play you the end of *The Ring*.

LEWIS: [*to* ZAC *as he heads off*] Zac, we don't have the time.

CHERRY: [*entering as Despina*] How do I look?

LEWIS: Good.

CHERRY: I'm having kittens and butterflies all at once.

JULIE: [*entering, wearing her costume*] Lewis, you'll have to speak to Roy.

LEWIS: What's the matter?

JULIE: He's leaving.

LEWIS: Leaving?

> [ROY *enters wearing normal clothes and carrying a suitcase*]

ROY: I'm not leaving, I'm quitting.

LEWIS: Where are you going, Roy?

ROY: Back to my ward, then I'll ask for a transfer to a closed ward.

LEWIS: But why?

ROY: It's for the best.

> [RUTH *enters wearing her costume.*]

LEWIS: But it was your dream to do *Così*.

ROY: Not any more.

RUTH: He's got stage fright.

ROY: Don't be ridiculous, woman.

RUTH: I saw you in the dressing room, talking to yourself, saying 'Come on, Roy, it'll be all right when you're on stage'.

ROY: She's got rabies. She's been bitten by Zac. Listen, I'm the only one here, besides Jerry, to have trod the boards. I don't get stage fright.

LEWIS: Why don't you do *Così* then?

ROY: Because I can't remember my lines. Not one. Gone.

CHERRY: That's stage fright.

ROY: It's not, it's a bad memory.

LEWIS: I know your lines, I'll whisper them to you.

ROY: People will hear.

CHERRY: They won't. I heard that the ward assistants are putting the doped up ones and catatonics in the front rows.

ROY: That's not going to help my performance. I feed off audience reaction!

[*Realising* ROY *is panicking,* LEWIS *leads him away to talk to him in private.*]

RUTH: [*to* JULIE, *taking the opportunity to go through the blocking*] Do we take six or seven steps in the garden scene? You know the one, where we give in to the boys when they're disguised. [*Starting to count out steps with a bemused* JULIE] One, two, three –

LEWIS: Roy, it's okay to have stage fright. I get it.

ROY: It's never happened to me before. Sweat. Dry mouth. Terminal memory loss.

LEWIS: I'll whisper the lines to you.

ROY: I can't. Can't. Can't do it.

LEWIS: Yes, you can.

ROY: Can't go on and make a fool of myself.

LEWIS: You won't.

ROY: Everyone will be staring at me!

LEWIS: That's the point, that's why you're on stage. If they didn't stare at you, I'd be worried.

ROY: Why?

LEWIS: It'd mean you weren't giving a good performance. I want you to be noticed all the time.

ROY: Generally that's what happens to me when I'm on stage. [*A beat.*] You're all right, Jerry.

[*To the others, exultant.*] I'm back!

[*As he hurries off, to* RUTH *and* JULIE] Let's go through some lines as I slip into my character.

[RUTH *and* JULIE *follow him out,* NICK *has entered unseen.*]

LEWIS: [to CHERRY] Are his parents coming tonight? Maybe that's why he's so nervous.

CHERRY: He hasn't got any parents, he's an orphan.

LEWIS: But I thought his mother and father –

CHERRY: He spent most of his early life in orphanages and being farmed out to foster parents who, realising what a nut case they had on their hands, put him back, quick smart.

NICK: Opening night nerves, Lewis?

LEWIS: Nick?

NICK: Didn't see you at the moratorium today.

LEWIS: Didn't have time. We only stopped rehearsing an hour ago.

NICK: You should have seen it!

[HENRY *enters wearing a tuxedo and his father's medals. He listens to* NICK *at a distance.*]

A hundred thousand people, maybe 200. Took hours to get to Parliament House, yelling out, '1, 2, 3, 4, we don't want your fuckin' war'. Radicalised the nation.

LEWIS: Why are you here?

NICK: Came to wish you the best for *Così.*

LEWIS: Why don't you stay and watch it?

NICK: Going out with Lucy to celebrate the moratorium.

LEWIS: She was coming to see this.

NICK: You don't understand, Lewis – today Australia was changed forever. She doesn't want to see an opera about a few upper class twits.

LEWIS: She said she was coming –

NICK: Lewis, we're mates, aren't we...?

[LEWIS *understands immediately.*]

LEWIS: You're sleeping with her!

NICK: No, she's sleeping with you, we're having sex.

LEWIS: In the same house.

NICK: Lucy's not possessive about you, I'm not possessive about her. What's the fuss?

LEWIS: Christ!

NICK: I thought you'd think the same. I didn't think you were so conservative.

LEWIS: [*half to himself*] Women's constancy is like an Arabian Phoenix.

NICK: What are you on about – too much time with the loonies, Lewis.

LEWIS: I should hit you.

NICK: Women shouldn't come between mates.

LEWIS: You're not my mate.

NICK: It's only sex.

LEWIS: Thanks a lot.

NICK: [*looking at* HENRY] Christ, medals too.

[*To* LEWIS] You have become a right wing nut, haven't you? You belong here.

[*He starts to sing*] They're coming to take me away, ha, ha, to the funny farm –

LEWIS: Don't sing that.

NICK: Why? It is a funny farm. [*Singing*] They're coming to take me away, ha, ha!

LEWIS: I said, don't sing that song!

[*He punches* NICK *to the floor.*]

NICK: You stupid bastard.

LEWIS: I said, don't sing that song.

NICK: That's all you are, a paper tiger.

[*He jumps up to hit* LEWIS, *but* HENRY *jumps in between them and grabs* NICK.]

HENRY: [*to* LEWIS] Do you want me to beat him until he can't stand up?

NICK: Let go!

HENRY: I can do it. I learnt it from the cops. I can do it without leaving bruises.

LEWIS: No, it's all right. [*To* NICK] Nick off.

NICK: Tres droll.

[HENRY *lets him go.*]

You know why Lucy left you for me? She said you were a lousy fuck.

[*He goes.*]

CHERRY: [*pleased*] Is that true, Lewis?

LEWIS: [*embarrassed*] I don't know – I mean she didn't tell me I was lousy –

CHERRY: I mean, is it true that your girlfriend has left you?

LEWIS: Yes.

CHERRY: [*pleased by the news*] Grouse. Double grouse.

> [*She gives him a peck on the cheek.*]

I dedicate my performance to you.

> [*She heads off, passing* JULIE *who is entering.*]
>
> [*Sotto voce, part threatening*] He's mine!
>
> [CHERRY *exits.*]

JULIE: Henry, Roy wants to go through his lines with you.

> [HENRY *nods and exits.*]

[*To* LEWIS] One minute he's in a panic the next he's an egomaniac. He says he wants a dressing room for himself.

LEWIS: We haven't got one.

JULIE: That's what I said.

> [RUTH *enters.*]

RUTH: He asked for our help then rejected it. No wonder D ward wants him transferred.

> [*She starts to map out her steps again.*]

One, two, three.

> [*She silently says her lines as she blocks out her part.*]

LEWIS: [*to* JULIE] I forgot to show you how to move those flats for the change. Around the back.

> [*They head off around the back.* ZAC *enters, still wearing the accordion.*]

ZAC: [*to* RUTH] Where's Lewis?

RUTH: Don't know. Damn. Mixed up my steps.

> [ZAC *looks around noticing no one is on stage. He goes over to* RUTH.]

ZAC: I suppose a fuck is out of the question?

> [*She slaps him across the face and stalks off.*]

A simple yes or no, would have been sufficient.

ROY: [*off, angrily*] Henry! Henry, you idiot!

ZAC: [*to himself*] Women. You have to wrap it all up in fancy
language and then they swoon for you, when all it comes
down to it the same thing.

[HENRY *comes running onto the stage.*]

Henry . . .

HENRY: Can't sssstop.

ZAC: I need a fuck.

HENRY: [*running on the spot*] Take a ppppill.

ZAC: I should, shouldn't I? I'm a bit nervous. You look a bit
nervous yourself.

HENRY: I mentioned *Macbeth* and Roy tried to strangle me. He
says I have to rrrrun around the theatre three times to get rid
of the curse.

[*He runs off.*]

ZAC: [*caught up in his own thoughts*] And they want foreplay.
[*Calling out as in golf*] Fore!
[*A beat.*] Too nervous. Too excited. All I wanted was a fuck
to calm me down.
[*He swallows a pill.*]
It's not as if it's the crown jewels or anything. Women are
God's punishment for men playing with themselves.
[HENRY *runs back across stage,* ZAC *pays no attention.*]
Wagner, do you hear me! I dedicate tonight to you! Fuck
Mozart, not one ounce of tragedy in him. Music for
elevators. Hmmmm, still too nervous. [*Swallowing a few
more pills*] That should do the trick.
[*He goes off humming the 'The Ride of the Valkyries'.*
JULIE *and* LEWIS *enter.*]

LEWIS: It's fairly easy, isn't it? Ruth will help you with that
large one during interval.
[*They stare at one another.*]
Nervous?

JULIE: A little. Not like giving a hair cut.
[*There are sounds of the doors opening and the audience
entering.*]

LEWIS: They're opening the doors.

JULIE: A kiss. A kiss for good luck.

> [*They kiss quickly. She laughs.*]

  Break a leg!

> [HENRY *runs on.*]

LEWIS: What is it, Henry?

HENRY: Cccccan't stop. Ggggot to break a curse!

LEWIS: Henry, the audience is coming in!

RUTH: [*running on stage*] Lewis!

LEWIS: What is it?

RUTH: Zac's on the floor in the dressing room. He's comatose!

> [JULIE *and* LEWIS *hurry off stage to* ZAC. HENRY *runs back on, a bit sweaty now.*]

HENRY: [*to himself, remembering lines*] Everyone blames women but I forgive them, if they change their love a thousand times a day, some call it sin, others a drug but I think it's the necessity of women's hearts.

> [*He runs off stage.*]

RUTH: [*entering*] Henry! [*To herself*] Now, where did he go?

> [*She hurries across the stage to look for him. He returns on the third circuit of his run and slows down mesmerised by seeing the audience for the first time.* RUTH *comes back on.*]

  Henry! We're skipping the overture. Come on, you're on!

> [*They exit.*]


## SCENE FOUR

---

*The theatre. It is in the final scene of the opera. Ferrando and Guglielmo are in their Australian military uniforms. Fiordiligi and Dorabella are there and Despina is with Don Alfonso.*

LEWIS:           We are safe and sound and have returned
                        from the war our hearts full of joy.

ROY:              Wanting to embrace our sweethearts

|  | and thank them for their fidelity. |
| HENRY: | Good heavens! Guglielmo. Ferrando! |
|  | Why are you back here? |
| LEWIS: | Recalled by royal command. |
| ROY: | Returned to our beautiful sweethearts |
| [*To* JULIE] | Why has the colour drained from your cheeks? |
| LEWIS: [*to* RUTH] | Why are you so upset? |
| ROY: | Why so silent? |
| HENRY: | They are tongue-tied with surprise. |
| JULIE: | My tongue has forsaken me. |
| RUTH: | If I don't die it'll be a miracle. |
| ROY: | Heavens, what do I see? |
|  | There's a man hidden in here! |
|  | A notary! |
|  | What's he doing there! |
| CHERRY: | No, sir. It's not a notary. |
|  | It's Despina, I'm just back from a fancy dress party. |
| LEWIS and ROY: | Could so clever a rogue ever be found? |
| DESPINA: | There's no one cleverer than me. |
| JULIE: | Despina! |
| RUTH: | Despina! |
| JULIE and RUTH: | What is happening? |

[HENRY *cunningly lets fall the contract signed by the women.*]

HENRY: [*sotto voce to the men*]

|  | I've dropped the papers. |

LEWIS: [*picking up the papers*]

|  | What are these papers? |
| ROY: | A marriage contract! |
| LEWIS: | Good god, you've signed here! |
| ROY: | And here! |
| LEWIS: | Where are these men? |
| ROY: | We'll kill them! |
| LEWIS: | We'll make these rooms flow with blood. |

[*They make to enter the other room, the women prevent them.*]

JULIE:            My love, my sin is mortal!

RUTH:           Kill me with your sword now!

LEWIS:          What is this all about?

JULIE: [*pointing to* HENRY *and* CHERRY]
                  Those two know.

HENRY:         Go into that room and you'll find out.

[*The men go into the room.*]

RUTH:           My blood runs cold.

[*From off-stage we hear* ROY *and* LEWIS *crying out as if savaging others.*]

LEWIS:          Take that!

ROY:            Take that you Albanian fiend!

JULIE:           I feel faint.

RUTH:           Oh, holy mother, I am weak.

[HENRY *and* CHERRY *catch the women before they fall to the floor in a faint; well they're supposed to, but* CHERRY, *still jealous of* JULIE, *lets her fall straight onto the floor. Then a cheerful* LEWIS *and* ROY *enter, wearing Albanian communist tops over their Australian uniforms.*]

LEWIS: [*to* RUTH] Lovely lady, a count of Albania bows
                  before you.

ROY: [*giving a miniature to* JULIE]
                  I return this miniature in lieu of your heart,
                  Madame.

WOMEN:        Heavens, what do we see?

MEN:            They're stupefied.

WOMEN:        I cannot bear this torment!

MEN:            They're half crazy.

JULIE and RUTH [*pointing to* HENRY]
                  This is the man who deceived us.

[*Everyone pauses. This is the music cue. They all look to where the music should be coming from, as* CHERRY *runs to the side of the stage and grabs giant cards on which the lyrics of the final song are written in English.*]

HENRY: [*sotto voce to* LEWIS] Where's my music?

JULIE: [*sotto voce to* LEWIS] Zac must be still out to it.

ROY: [*sotto voce*] Someone faint.

RUTH: I'm not supposed to faint.

ROY: [*sotto voce*] Henry, faint.

HENRY: [*not wanting to dirty his clothes*] My tuxedo will get dirty.

> [ROY *clutches his chest, pretending to have a heart attack.*
> LEWIS *runs off stage to put on the record.*]

ROY: Get me the musicians or I'll die! [*He collapses onto the floor.*]

> [*To* RUTH.] See what your infidelity has done to me!

>> [*The music starts up, surprising everyone at the suddenness of it, except* HENRY. *He immediately gets into his stride, half miming, half singing the Italian lyrics.* CHERRY *shows the cue cards to the audience so they can sing along.*]

HENRY:          I deceived you but my deception
                undeceived your lovers who,
                from now on will be wiser.
                Give me your hands, now that you're united
                Embrace each other and say no more about
                    it
                All four of you can laugh now
                as I have laughed and will continue to
                    laugh.

> [HENRY *takes over* CHERRY's *job of showing the English translation while the others get into the swing of miming to the Italian lyrics.*]

JULIE: and RUTH:    My love, if this is true
                    I will compensate your heart
                    with love and with fidelity
                    and will love you forever

LEWIS and ROY:      I believe you, my beautiful one,
                    But I won't put you to the test again

CHERRY:             Is this a dream

.

ALL:

I'm confused and ashamed
But doesn't matter if they fooled me
because I'll fool others
Happy is the man who calmly takes life as
    he finds it
and through the vicissitudes of life
lets himself be ruled by reason
what makes another weep
will make him laugh
and despite the tempests of his life
he will find serenity and peace

## SCENE FIVE

---

*The theatre. The performance is over.* LEWIS, *tired and sweaty but pleased, is talking to* JUSTIN, *who shakes his hand.*

JUSTIN: Marvellous. Just marvellous, Lewis. Everyone thoroughly enjoyed it. A few down the front were a bit quiet, but what can you expect from catatonics, right? And the cast! Didn't think it was possible. Came right out of their shells. They blossomed. Blossomed!

LEWIS: Yes, they did. The only problem we had was Zac. Too much medication. He woke up at interval and went back to his ward.

JUSTIN: The other good thing is that you proved Roy wrong.

LEWIS: What do you mean?

JUSTIN: Every day after rehearsals he came and complained to me about your direction. I said 'Lewis will come through' and you did!

LEWIS: [*irritated*] Every day?

JUSTIN: Oh, yes, regular as clockwork. [*Spotting* RUTH *who has changed, entering*] Ah, Ruth. Marvellous. Just marvellous!

RUTH: I missed a couple of things. I should have done four steps instead of five in that section where Julie and I –

LEWIS: [*stopping her*] You were fine, Ruth. Fine.

JUSTIN: Well, goodnight, Lewis [*Shoving a small envelope in* LEWIS' *palm*] Your pay packet –

RUTH: [*shaking* LEWIS*'s hand*] Thank you, I really liked it.

LEWIS: Good.

RUTH: I hate goodbyes, so when the others come out tell them I'm waiting outside counting the stars.

LEWIS: Okay.

> [LEWIS *unbuttons his army top, smiling and singing to himself the final aria of* Così.]
>> Fortunato l'uom che prende
>> Ogni cosa pel buon verso
>
> [DOUG *appears, his face covered in bandages.*]

Doug.

DOUG: The one and only.

LEWIS: You were here?

DOUG: At the back with the schizos. Been released from C ward. On my best behaviour. How's the girlfriend?

LEWIS: Lucy and I aren't together anymore.

DOUG: I meant Julie. She a good root, is she?

LEWIS: Doug, will you stop talking like that?

DOUG: This theatre would have burnt like a real beauty. [*A beat.*] My motto is to try and try again. Work at it until you succeed. My mother instilled in me a Protestant work ethnic.

LEWIS: Don't you have to be back in your ward?

DOUG: Trying to get rid of me, mate? You should have done a Little Richard opera. I thought you were lousy in my role by the way.

LEWIS: Thanks, Doug.

DOUG: A bit sissy. Personally, I think you're a closet fag. I would have given Ferrando balls. [CHERRY *comes in and watches them.*] So, you're no longer with Lucy. She a good fuck? Might visit her, give her the old pork rattlesnake. You said she was into free love, didn't you? Can't get over it.

You do this old fashioned opera – this is the era of free love
and orgies. See, ya. [*To* CHERRY] Bye, fat dog.

CHERRY: Go burn a cat.

DOUG: [*to* CHERRY] Who writes your lines? Oscar Wilde?
[*At exit*] I have only one word for you, Lewis –
Awopbopalooboplopbamboo! [*He goes.*]

CHERRY: He's jealous because he didn't perform tonight. Say,
ah! Go on, pretend I'm a doctor. Say, ah!

LEWIS: Ah –

> [*In saying it* LEWIS *opens his mouth and* CHERRY *thrusts
> a chocolate liqueur down it.*]

CHERRY: Cherry brandy chocolate liqueur. Bought it for you.
Like paradise, eh? [*He nods to please her.*] Here's a love
letter. There'll be plenty more where that came from. Doug
gave me your address. I love chocolate. Give me a kiss. No,
open your mouth, I want a tonguey. [*She slaps him on the
cheek, his mouth automatically opens and she kisses him
long and passionately*] Hmmmmm, lovely. Chocolate.
[HENRY *enters*] I'm going to miss you, lover boy. But once
I'm out of here, it'll be wham, bam, thank you, Lewis. I
better go before I start crying.

> [*She goes and* HENRY *comes over to* LEWIS *and shakes his
> hand. This time with his left hand because his right hand
> is now paralysed.*]

HENRY: Ttttthank you.

LEWIS: Thank you, Henry. Hey, your right arm is paralysed, it
used to be your left one.

HENRY: It changes.

> [*He goes.* LEWIS *continues to undress, taking off the top
> half of his army jacket and putting on a clean shirt.* JULIE
> *enters and watches him for a time.*]

JULIE: Nice bod.

> [*He smiles, pleased to see her.*]

We had them in the palm of our hand.

> [*She laughs.*]

LEWIS: You're very happy.

JULIE: I enjoyed tonight. Also, I'm in good spirits because I'm leaving this place.

LEWIS: You're leaving the institution?

JULIE: Yep. Flying the coop next Thursday. Then straight out of here and the first train to Sydney.

LEWIS: [*disappointed*] Sydney? [*A beat.*] I can take you to the railway station if you like.

JULIE: I don't know if you should.

LEWIS: Why?

JULIE: I think I fell for you.

LEWIS: What's the matter with that?

JULIE: I need something stable in my life. I need my girlfriend. She's stood by me, through thick and thin, mostly thin. She's coming up to Sydney with me.

    [LEWIS *now understands.*]

Without her I would be dead. I do like you. I do. You'll visit me before I go, will you?

LEWIS: Of course.

JULIE: I'd like that. But not when my girlfriend's here. She gets terribly jealous. [*Kissing him on the cheek*] Au revoir.

CHERRY: [*entering, she sees the kiss*] Hey, slut!

    [*She takes out her pocket knife.*]

I'm going to fix you once and for all!

LEWIS: Cherry...

CHERRY: [*advancing on* JULIE] Don't try to talk me out of killing her, Lewis, I'm going to do womankind a favour.

    [LEWIS *jumps in between* CHERRY *and* JULIE.]

LEWIS: Cherry –

    [*He grabs her in an embrace and kisses her passionately. The fingers holding the knife gradually loosen and the knife falls to the floor.*]

CHERRY: [*dazed*] Wow...

    [LEWIS *bends down and picks up the pocket knife and puts it in his pocket.*]

A keepsake, eh?

LEWIS: Yes.

CHERRY: Sorry, my emotions got the better of me. Will you tell
     Roy to get a hurry on? Ruth is driving us mad out there with
     her counting. She's up to two thousand stars all ready.
          [JULIE *walks past* CHERRY *on the way out.*]
JULIE: [*referring to* LEWIS] He's the best lay I've ever had.
          [*She holds out her hands to indicate a huge cock size.*]
     It's gi-normous.
          [*She goes laughing.*]
CHERRY: You two didn't?
LEWIS: She was only joking. [*Ruefully*] Teasing you.
CHERRY: Good, because I would have had to kill you or her
     otherwise. Love letter in the post tomorrow, lover.
          [ROY *enters wearing a crimson smoking jacket and
          smoking a cigarette with a cigarette holder.*]
     Hurry up.
ROY: Be there in a mo, darling.
          [CHERRY *goes.*]
     Well, Jerry, we did it.
LEWIS: Certainly did. Though I hear you had your doubts. Justin
     said you complained about my direction.
ROY: You do have a few teething problems with your direction.
     I made up a list of them. [*Giving a list to* LEWIS] I know that
     you can take criticism because you must get a lot of it.
LEWIS: [*reading the list*] 'Always use the word please and thank
     you when addressing the cattle, after all, they're not actors'.
ROY: Got it back to front. Bit of a rush. You know what I mean
     anyway. Read it at home. It's rather comprehensive and it
     could be an instructive couple of hours.
LEWIS: Thank you, Roy.
ROY: Pleasure. Back to D ward. I noticed some of the wildest
     applause come from the D ward section tonight. I expect a
     surprise party for me. I'll act surprised. Should I be wildly
     surprised, like this? [*Demonstrating*] Or be so astonished that
     I'm stunned?
LEWIS: Stunned.

ROY: I might do the opposite. The reasons for me not taking
your advice are on that list. [*Shaking his hand*] Next year, a
greater triumph awaits us, Jerry. The Don!

LEWIS: The Don?

ROY: *Don Giovanni*. Time for me to go beyond these ensemble
pieces, time for a lead role. Humility can limit you. I was
once a lady-killer in my time. [*Whispering*] Literally.

   [*He laughs. He goes out trying out his wildly enthusiastic
   expressions of surprise.*]

For me?! Oh, you boys of D ward, what a bunch of hi jinks
guys you are. [*Stops*] Jerry, turn off the lights on your way
out.

LEWIS: [*bemused*] Yes, Roy.

   [ROY *goes.*]

[*addressing the audience*] There was no next year. This
theatre mysteriously burnt down a week after the
performance and Doug was the major suspect. I shifted
house soon after *Così* and so I only got one love letter from
Cherry, who told me to think of her every time I played with
the flick knife. Lucy and Nick? Well they didn't last long as
both were not into fidelity. Lucy became an academic and
Nick became a Labour MP in the Upper House. Ruth left the
institution to become a time and motion expert. Henry? He
died soon after *Così*. Roy? He went from ward to ward after
his fellow patients took up petitions to get rid of him. By the
following year I was in Sydney and not long after that I saw
Julie's name in the paper. She had died of a drug overdose.
And Zac? He left the asylum and founded a rock and roll
group called The Psychotic Wagners. They had a minor hit.
A few years later I heard he had started a polka band which
was very big in the Melbourne German and Austrian club
circuit. [*A beat.*] Time to turn out the lights.

   [*He turns off the lights. Blackout.*]


## THE END

## ALSO BY LOUIS NOWRA FROM CURRENCY PRESS

**PLAYS**

> *Capricornia*
> *Crow*
> *The Golden Age*
> *The Incorruptible*
> *Inner Voices / Albert Names Edward*
> *Inside the Island / The Precious Woman*
> *The Language of the Gods*
> *Radiance*
> *Summer of the Aliens*
> *Sunrise*
> *The Temple*
> *Visions*

**SCREENPLAYS**

> *Così*

## ABOUT LOUIS NOWRA

*The Theatre of Louis Nowra*, by Veronica Kelly,

Louis Nowra's work is highly theatrical, blackly comic and draws on references from Ovid and Shakespeare to horror movies and tabloid newspapers. In her compelling study, Veronica Kelly draws out the sources of Nowra's passionate, idiosyncratic vision and demonstrates how it reveals the turbulence at the root of Australian history.

Veronica Kelly is Associate Professor in Drama in the English Department of Queensland University. The book includes a full list of Nowra's works and a select bibliography.

For a full list of our titles, visit our website:

# www.currency.com.au

Currency Press
The performing arts publisher
PO Box 2287
Strawberry Hills NSW 2012
Australia
currency@magna.com.au
Tel: (02) 9319 5877
Fax: (02) 9319 3649

THE LEARNING RESOURCE CENTRE
HERSCHEL GRAMMAR SCHOOL
NORTHAMPTON AVENUE
SLOUGH          SL1 3BW

WITHDRAWN